Big Apple Almanac 3

by Patrick M. Reynolds

Published by

The Red Rose Studio
Willow Street, PA 17584

Introduction

Big Apple Almanac is a fact-based cartoon that highlights incidents, and characters that somehow fell through the cracks of New York City's history. The feature originates in the comics section of **New York Newsday** every Sunday. It also appears in the **Staten Island Advance.**

Each page in this book is a reproduction of a weekly installment of **Big Apple Almanac** with added paragraphs of copy that enhance the stories.

This book is divided into two parts. The first section contains assorted stories about New York City arranged chronologically. The last part, starting on page 78, features anecdotes from the history of sports in New York.

Contents

About the Author-Artist

Patrick M. Reynolds started doing cartoons of little-known historical anecdotes in 1976 with **Pennsylvania Profiles.** That feature ran for over fifteen years in newspapers across the Keystone State. Currently he does all the research, writing, and artwork for **Big Apple Almanac** along with two other weekly cartoons, **Texas Lore** and **Flashbacks.**

Originally from Minersville, PA, Patrick earned a Bachelor of Fine Arts Degree from Pratt Institute in Brooklyn and a Masters Degree in Illustration from Syracuse University. He now lives in Lancaster County, Pennsylvania with his wife, Patricia, and children: Kimberly Jo, Maria Alyssa, and Thomas Patrick.

FLASHBACKS by Patrick M. Reynolds

How the White House Got Its Name

This is a sample of Mr. Reynolds' cartoon, **Flashbacks**, which appears in **The Washington Post**. Other newspapers which carry this feature are the **Harrisburg Patriot-News, Greensburg Tribune-Review, Erie Times-News,** and **Pottsville Republican** - all in Pennsylvania.

The systematic digging of wells on New York's public streets was begun in 1677 by Common Council. However, the geological formation of lower Manhattan was not favorable for obtaining good water; the taste was brackish, and the lack of a sewer system made it even worse. Finally, the supply was subject to varying levels on account of the weather.

The Tea Water Pump

Near Bethune (now West 4th St.) was a spring of exceptionally pure water owned by a Mr. Knapp who sold it from carts. The New York City Directory of 1796 lists 21 proprietors of Tea Water Carts - none of them were licensed.

DURING THE 17th AND 18th CENTURIES, NEW YORKERS GOT THEIR WATER FROM SPRINGS BENEATH THE CITY. PUMPS WERE ERECTED ON STREET CORNERS ABOUT EVERY FOUR BLOCKS, BUT THIS WATER TASTED AWFUL.

THE MOST CELEBRATED PUMP IN THE CITY WAS ON PRESENT-DAY PARK ROW NEAR PEARL STREET. THE SPARKLING PURITY OF THIS WATER WAS CONSIDERED IDEAL FOR MAKING THE PEOPLES' FAVORITE DRINK—TEA. HENCE, IT WAS CALLED *THE TEA WATER PUMP.*

TO SAVE PEOPLE THE TIME AND STRAIN OF LUGGING PAILS OF WATER MANY BLOCKS TO THEIR HOMES, SOME ENTREPRENEURS FILLED BARRELS WITH "TEA WATER" AND PEDDLED IT AROUND TOWN FOR TWO CENTS A BUCKET-FULL.

AS THE CROTON WATER SYSTEM EXPANDED IN THE 19th CENTURY, THE CITY REMOVED THE STREET PUMPS. THE *TEA WATER PUMP* VANISHED FROM THE SCENE BY 1829.

An official volunteer fire department for New York City was organized in 1737 when the General Assembly of the Colony passed a law which required Common Council to select certain "...strong, able, discreet, honest, and sober men..." not to exceed forty in number, to be called Firemen of the City of New York.

NEW YORK'S FIRST FIRE ENGINES

NEW YORK'S VOLUNTEER FIREMEN FOUGHT FIRES WITH BUCKETS, HOOKS, AND CHAINS UNTIL THE FIRST FIRE ENGINES ARRIVED FROM RICHARD NEWSHAM'S FACTORY, LONDON, ENGLAND IN DECEMBER, 1731.

FOR WEEKS PEOPLE CAME FROM ALL OVER TO ADMIRE THE NEW ENGINES HOUSED IN SHEDS BEHIND CITY HALL. NUMBER ONE WAS ON THE EAST AND NUMBER TWO WAS ON THE WEST FACING WHAT IS NOW NASSAU STREET.

THE CITY'S WEALTHIEST AND MOST POWERFUL CITIZENS COMPRISED THESE FIRST FIRE ENGINE COMPANIES. TWO OVERSEERS OF ENGINE No. TWO WERE BROTHERS, NICHOLAS AND JOHN ROOSEVELT.

The town of Philipsburgh, NY takes its name from a Manor established in 1680 by the Philipse family. The land was originally leased from the Dutch West India Company.

Over the years the Philipse holdings grew because of some shrewdly arranged marriages. Eventually, the Philipse Estate covered most of what is now Putnam County.

New York's First Toll Bridge

THE **PHILIPSE** FAMILY, LAND RICH ARISTOCRATS IN WESTCHESTER, RECEIVED A FRANCHISE FROM THE CROWN IN 1693 TO CONSTRUCT A BRIDGE ACROSS THE HARLEM RIVER.

NAMED **KINGSBRIDGE** AFTER WILLIAM OF ORANGE (KING WILLIAM III), IT STOOD AT 230th STREET AND BROADWAY.

FARMERS FROM UPPER MANHATTAN AND THE BRONX PAID THE PHILIPSES UP TO **15 POUNDS** STERLING A YEAR TO TAKE THEIR **PRODUCE** ACROSS THE BRIDGE TO MARKETS IN NEW YORK CITY.

IN 1756 JOHN PALMER LED A GROUP OF IRATE CITIZENS IN A PROTEST OVER THE PHILIPSE'S UNFAIR TOLLS.

YOU MISER, WE'LL BUILD OUR OWN TOLL-FREE BRIDGE!

NOT WANTING ANY COMPETITION, THE INFLUENTIAL FREDERICK PHILIPSE GOT THE BRITISH ARMY TO DRAFT PALMER TO FIGHT IN THE FRENCH & INDIAN WAR.

Greetings!

BUT PALMER PAID SOMEONE TO TAKE HIS PLACE.

The Philipse Castle, built in 1683, was the earlier of two houses on the estate. It stands today at 381 Bellwood Avenue in Tarrytown. The second grand house was the Manor, built in 1745 at present day 29 Warburton Avenue, Yonkers.

The Bridge Squabble

Parts of the Phlipse Estate still stand and are open to the public.

FREDERICK PHILIPSE OPERATED A TOLL BRIDGE ACROSS THE HARLEM RIVER IN 1756.

JOHN PALMER AND OTHER CITIZENS GOT FED UP WITH PHILIPSE'S HIGH TOLLS.

SO THEY STARTED TO BUILD THEIR OWN TOLL-FREE BRIDGE.

AGAIN PHILIPSE GOT PALMER DRAFTED INTO THE BRITISH ARMY, AND **AGAIN** PALMER PAID A MERCENARY TO TAKE HIS PLACE.

PALMER'S TOLL-FREE BRIDGE WAS FINALLY COMPLETED IN 1758.

IT STOOD AT 225th ST. & BROADWAY.

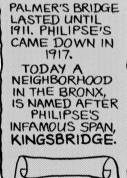

AROUND 1786, AFTER THE REVOLUTIONARY WAR, THE U.S. GOVERNMENT CONFISCATED PHILIPSE'S ESTATE BECAUSE HE WAS A TORY. HIS FORMER BRIDGE WAS MADE TOLL-FREE.

PALMER'S BRIDGE LASTED UNTIL 1911. PHILIPSE'S CAME DOWN IN 1917.

TODAY A NEIGHBORHOOD IN THE BRONX IS NAMED AFTER PHILIPSE'S INFAMOUS SPAN, **KINGSBRIDGE.**

The money required for the founding of King's College was raised by the Provincial Assembly through a public lottery. The first president was Dr. Samuel Johnson, an Anglican minister from Stratford, Connecticut. Until the building shown in the last panel was finished, classes were held in the schoolhouse of Trinity Church.

KING'S COLLEGE

The first class consisted of eight men from some of New York's oldest families including Verplanck, Van Cortlandt, and Bayard.

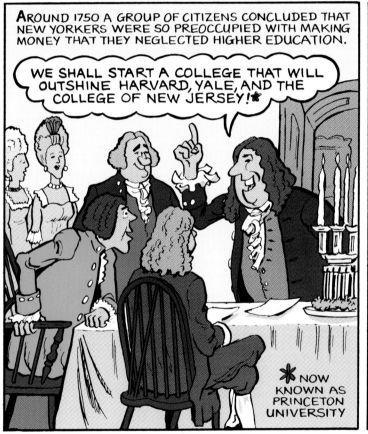

AROUND 1750 A GROUP OF CITIZENS CONCLUDED THAT NEW YORKERS WERE SO PREOCCUPIED WITH MAKING MONEY THAT THEY NEGLECTED HIGHER EDUCATION.

WE SHALL START A COLLEGE THAT WILL OUTSHINE HARVARD, YALE, AND THE COLLEGE OF NEW JERSEY!*

* NOW KNOWN AS PRINCETON UNIVERSITY

AMONG THESE INTELLECTUALS WERE SOME VESTRYMEN OF **TRINITY CHURCH** WHO ARRANGED FOR THE TRANSFER OF FIVE ACRES OF CHURCH PROPERTY BOUNDED BY CHURCH, MURRAY, AND BARCLAY, EXTENDING TO THE HUDSON RIVER.

KING GEORGE II GRANTED THE CHARTER IN 1754, AND THE COUNTRY'S SIXTH UNIVERSITY WAS CALLED KING'S COLLEGE. THE CORNERSTONE WAS LAID IN 1756 AND IT TOOK FOUR YEARS TO ERECT THE MAIN BUILDING AT PARK PLACE.

AFTER THE REVOLUTIONARY WAR, ITS NAME WAS CHANGED TO **COLUMBIA UNIVERSITY.**

The Mohican Indians originally called this island *Minnissais*, meaning "lesser island."

BECAUSE OF THE MOLLUSKS FOUND THERE, THE DUTCH COLONISTS NAMED A 12 ACRE ISLAND IN NEW YORK BAY

OYSTER ISLAND.

IN 1670 FRANCIS LOVELACE TOOK OVER AS GOVERNOR OF NEW YORK AND RENAMED SEVERAL PLACES AFTER HIMSELF. OYSTER ISLAND BECAME **LOVE ISLAND.**

A YEAR LATER THERE WAS A FOOD SHORTAGE, SO GOVERNOR LOVELACE APPOINTED A PROMINENT DUTCHMAN, **ISAAC BEDLOE**, AS THE CHIEF FOOD PROCURER FOR NEW YORK CITY.

BEDLOE REQUIRED ALL SHIPS TO STOP AT LOVE ISLAND TO BE INSPECTED. AS A RESULT, BEDLOE PUT A STOP TO THE SMUGGLING AND BLACK-MARKETING OF FOOD.

AFTER THE CRISIS ENDED, GOV. LOVELACE EXPRESSED HIS APPRECIATION BY PRESENTING A DEED FOR THE ISLAND TO MR. BEDLOE, AND RENAMING IT **BEDLOE'S ISLAND.**

State of New York
Deed

ISAAC BEDLO

TWO CENTURIES LATER, BEDLOE'S ISLAND ACHIEVED WORLD FAME WHEN IT BECAME THE HOME OF THE **STATUE OF LIBERTY.**

The Spaniards were harassing British slave ships in the Caribbean Sea, so both countries went to war in the 1730's. This was Peter Warren's baptism of fire.

He next saw action in King George's War (1742-48) which was one of several conflicts between France and England for domination of North America.

Peter Warren,

A CAPTAIN IN THE BRITISH NAVY, SANK OR CAPTURED TWO DOZEN ENEMY SPANISH AND FRENCH SHIPS DURING THE 1730'S & 40'S. ONE WAS CARRYING GOLD AND SILVER WORTH £250,000.

IN THOSE DAYS AN OFFICER'S SALARY INCLUDED A PERCENTAGE OF THE BOOTY HE CAPTURED.

CPT. WARREN OFTEN LANDED IN NEW YORK WHERE HE HIRED STEPHEN DE LANCEY'S FIRM TO SELL HIS LOOT.

BETWEEN 1731 AND 1744 WARREN PURCHASED OVER 300 ACRES ON THE WEST SIDE OF NEW YORK. IT WAS THE LARGEST ESTATE EVER IN GREENWICH VILLAGE.

ALONG THE WAY PETER MARRIED DE LANCEY'S DAUGHTER, SUSANNAH.

William Cosby was governor of New York from 1732 to 1736 during which time he accumulated 14,000 acres for himself along the Mohawk River. Cosby's Chief Justice was James De Lancey, the brother-in-law of Peter Warren. When Governor Cosby died, James helped Peter purchase Cosby's estate for a mere one hundred ten pounds.

Greenwich Village's Admiral

Warrensburg near Lake George was named after Sir Peter Warren.

BY 1744 CAPTAIN PETER WARREN OF THE BRITISH NAVY OWNED OVER 300 ACRES IN GREENWICH VILLAGE. HE BUILT A MANSION ON A HILL NEAR PRESENT-DAY CHARLES AND BLEECKER STREETS, WITH A VIEW OF STATEN ISLAND AND THE NEW JERSEY HIGHLANDS. SHOWN HERE IS WARREN AND HIS WIFE, THE FORMER SUSANNAH DE LANCEY.

CAPTAIN WARREN WAS OFTEN OUT OF TOWN DOING THE KING'S BUSINESS—BLASTING FRENCH SHIPS AND FORTS. THEN, IN 1745...

FOR KNOCKING OFF THE FRENCH FORT, LOUISBERG IN NOVA SCOTIA, HE WAS KNIGHTED AND PROMOTED TO ADMIRAL.

TWO YEARS LATER SIR PETER WAS ELECTED TO REPRESENT WESTMINSTER IN PARLIAMENT.

HE LEFT NEW YORK, NEVER TO RETURN. THE ADMIRAL DIED IN 1752 AND WAS BURIED IN...

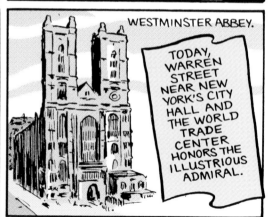

WESTMINSTER ABBEY.

TODAY, WARREN STREET NEAR NEW YORK'S CITY HALL AND THE WORLD TRADE CENTER HONORS THE ILLUSTRIOUS ADMIRAL.

As governor, the Earl of Bellomont's main problems were enforcing the trade laws and protecting New York merchants and ship owners from pirates such as William Kidd.

He did, however, manage to introduce a few improvements to the city: street lighting, a new city hall, establishment of a night watch, and this, the first library.

New York's First Public Library

THE EARL OF BELLOMONT'S* CHAPLAIN, REV. JOHN SHARP, STARTED THE FIRST PUBLIC LIBRARY IN NEW YORK WHEN, IN 1700, HE DONATED HIS COLLECTION OF BOOKS TO THE CITY. THEY WERE HOUSED IN CITY HALL (NOW FEDERAL HALL ON WALL ST.).

* GOVERNOR OF NEW YORK, 1698 TO 1701.

IN 1754 SOME PROMINENT NEW YORKERS ORGANIZED AN ASSOCIATION TO MANAGE REV. SHARP'S COLLECTION WHICH THEY NAMED THE CITY LIBRARY.

THE NOTORIOUS KING GEORGE III ISSUED A CHARTER IN 1772 WHICH OFFICIALLY DESIGNATED THIS ASSOCIATION AS THE NEW YORK SOCIETY LIBRARY.

OVER THE YEARS THE LIBRARY HAS MOVED SEVERAL TIMES.

WHEN NEW YORK WAS THE CAPITAL OF THE U.S. (1789-90), THIS LIBRARY SERVED AS THE FIRST LIBRARY OF CONGRESS.

TODAY THE NEW YORK SOCIETY LIBRARY HAS OVER 185,000 BOOKS AND IS STILL OPEN TO THE PUBLIC AT 53 E. 79th ST.

At first, there was no genuine "printers' union." The Journeymen typesetters merely got together and selected a committee to visit the shop owners with their list of demands.

Depicted here is a print shop owner meeting with a printers' committee.

Collective Bargaining

IN 1778 THE JOURNEYMEN PRINTERS OF NEW YORK NEGOTIATED A RAISE IN PAY. THIS WAS THE FIRST RECORDED ATTEMPT IN THE UNITED STATES BY AN ORGANIZED GROUP OF WORKERS TO BARGAIN WITH THEIR EMPLOYERS.

AFTER THE REVOLUTIONARY WAR, IN 1794, THE CITY'S PRINTERS FORMED THE TYPOGRAPHICAL SOCIETY WHICH WON FOR THEM A WAGE OF ONE DOLLAR A DAY.

ALTHOUGH IT HAS BEEN REORGANIZED SEVERAL TIMES, THE TYPOGRAPHICAL UNION IS ONE OF THE OLDEST UNIONS IN THE COUNTRY.

The first session of the U. S. Supreme Court lasted two days. Day One was all pomp and ceremony. The primary business on Day Two was the reading of the justices' commissions and fixing a penalty of imprisonment for anyone who did not keep quiet during the reading.

WIGS AND ROBES

John Jay was 44 when he was appointed as the first Chief Justice of the U.S. Supreme Court in 1789. His only experience on the bench was as Chief Justice of New York from 1775 to 1777.

THE SUPREME COURT OF THE U.S. HELD ITS FIRST MEETING ON FEBRUARY 1, 1790 IN THE ROYAL EXCHANGE BUILDING AT THE FOOT OF BROAD STREET.

PRESIDENT WASHINGTON HAD APPOINTED SIX JUSTICES, BUT ONLY THREE SHOWED UP FOR THE OPENING SESSION. THEY WERE, FROM LEFT: WILLIAM CUSHING OF BOSTON, CHIEF JUSTICE JOHN JAY OF NEW YORK, AND JAMES WILSON OF PHILADELPHIA.

AFTER THE NEXT DAY'S BUSINESS, JUSTICE CUSHING WAS WALKING DOWN BROADWAY TO HIS LODGINGS WHEN A MOB OF BOYS STARTED TO FOLLOW AND TEASE HIM.

LOOK AT THE SILLY BRITISH WIG!

HEY, SHEEP-HEAD!

WITH THAT, CUSHING STOPPED WEARING A WIG AND SOON OTHER JUDGES FOLLOWED SUIT.

AMERICAN JUDGES FINALLY STOPPED WEARING WIGS WHEN, AROUND 1801, PRESIDENT THOMAS JEFFERSON QUIPPED...

IF YOU JUDGES INSIST ON WEARING THOSE BRITISH ROBES, FOR HEAVEN'S SAKE DISCARD THE MONSTROUS WIGS WHICH MAKE ENGLISH JUDGES LOOK LIKE RATS PEEPING THROUGH BUNCHES OF OAKUM.

Yellow fever was common in the early days of New York. There were no records kept but, in 1798, 20 doctors died fighting it.

The Yellow Fever Hospital

In 1816 new Almshouse buildings were completed on the site of the farm in this story.

LINDLEY MURRAY MADE A BUNDLE AS A MERCHANT AND WRITER OF GRAMMAR TEXTBOOKS BEFORE THE REVOLUTIONARY WAR. HE BOUGHT A FARM ALONG THE EAST RIVER FROM PRESENT-DAY 24th to 28th STREETS AND NAMED IT BELLE VUE.

AFTER THE WAR MURRAY DECIDED TO RETIRE AND MOVE TO ENGLAND, SO HE SOLD HIS PLACE TO BROCKHOLST LIVINGSTON.

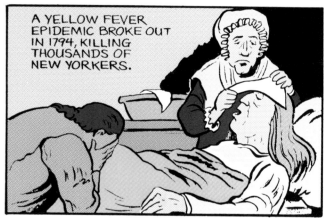

A YELLOW FEVER EPIDEMIC BROKE OUT IN 1794, KILLING THOUSANDS OF NEW YORKERS.

GOVERNOR DEWITT CLINTON ASKED SEVERAL PROMINENT CITIZENS TO DEAL WITH THE EMERGENCY.

THIS COMMITTEE LEASED LIVINGSTON'S FARM AND CARED FOR YELLOW FEVER VICTIMS IN THE FARMHOUSE.

THE CITY PURCHASED THE FARM OUTRIGHT IN 1798, AND THAT WAS THE BEGINNING OF BELLEVUE HOSPITAL.

Early life insurance policies were issued for short periods under very rigid restrictions. A policy could be revoked for many reasons such as non-payment of a premium, suicide of the insured, any false statement on the application, death on the high seas, death in a duel, death at the hands of the law, and death while in the Army or Navy.

Policy Peddlers

One of the strangest reasons for revoking a life insurance policy in the years before the Civil War was for living or traveling anywhere south of Virginia and Kentucky between July 1st and November 1st.

AT FIRST, LIFE INSURANCE WAS AVAILABLE ON A COME-AND-GET-IT BASIS, AND HARDLY ANYONE BOTHERED TO GET IT. THERE WERE LESS THAN 100 LIFE POLICIES IN THE COUNTRY IN 1800.

THE INDUSTRY WAS REVOLUTIONIZED BY THE NEW YORK LIFE INSURANCE & TRUST CO., SHOWN HERE AT 52 WALL ST.

NEW YORK LIFE'S FOUNDER (IN 1830) & FIRST PRESIDENT, WILLIAM BARD, CAME UP WITH THE IDEA OF ACTIVELY SELLING LIFE INSURANCE.

MR. BARD APPOINTED PHYSICIANS, LAWYERS, MERCHANTS, TRADESMEN, AND OTHER REPUTABLE BUSINESSMEN AS LOCAL AGENTS.

HE SUPPLIED EACH WITH PAMPHLETS EXPLAINING LIFE INSURANCE, APPLICATION FORMS, AND A SMALL ADVERTISING ALLOWANCE. ALTHOUGH BARD PAID THEM A FIVE PERCENT COMMISSION,

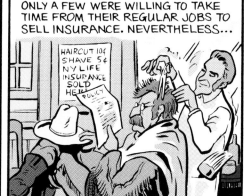

ONLY A FEW WERE WILLING TO TAKE TIME FROM THEIR REGULAR JOBS TO SELL INSURANCE. NEVERTHELESS...

HAIRCUT 10¢
SHAVE 5¢
NY LIFE INSURANCE SOLD HERE
POLICY

AT THE END OF ONE YEAR, BARD'S COMPANY HAD SOLD 1,821 LIFE POLICIES.

OTHER FIRMS TOOK NOTICE AND BEGAN TO HIRE AGENTS.

One of the writers mentioned in this story, James K. Paulding, was very popular during the first quarter of the 19th century. He published *The New Pilgrim's Progress*, a satire on the guidebooks and writings of English travelers, and a parody on fashionable life in New York City.

THE CITY'S UNOFFICIAL NICKNAME

IN 1807 THREE YOUNG MEN— **WASHINGTON IRVING,** HIS BROTHER WILLIAM, AND JAMES KIRKE PAULDING — WROTE STORIES POKING FUN AT THE RIDICULOUSLY FORMAL MANNERS OF THEIR FELLOW NEW YORKERS.

THESE ESSAYS WERE PRINTED IN A SMALL PAMPHLET ENTITLED *SALMAGUNDI.*

SALMAGUNDI WAS A **HASH** MADE OF MINCED VEAL, PICKLED HERRING, ANCHOVIES, AND ONIONS SERVED WITH OIL AND LEMON JUICE.

THE AUTHORS OF *SALMAGUNDI* REFERRED TO NEW YORK AS *GOTHAM* BECAUSE OF AN EVENT IN THE ENGLISH VILLAGE OF GOTHAM IN THE 13th CENTURY.

IT SEEMED THAT KING JOHN PLANNED TO BUY A CASTLE IN GOTHAM. FIGURING THEY'D HAVE TO TAKE CARE OF THE KING'S ESTATE...

THE VILLAGERS DECIDED TO ACT LIKE IDIOTS AND SCARE AWAY THE KING.   IT WORKED.

ON SEEING THEIR SILLY ANTICS, THE KING WANTED NO PART OF GOTHAM.

MANY NEW YORKERS ADOPTED *GOTHAM* AS THEIR CITY'S NICKNAME, UNAWARE THAT IRVING AND PAULDING MEANT IT AS *A PLACE FOR SLY FOOLS.*

14

Both before and after the Revolutionary War, William Street was the dry-goods section of New York.

The Street With Many Names

Delmonico's restaurant on William Street burned down in 1835. The brothers moved their business to 76 Broad Street until construction was finished on their new building at the intersection of Beaver, William, and South William Streets.

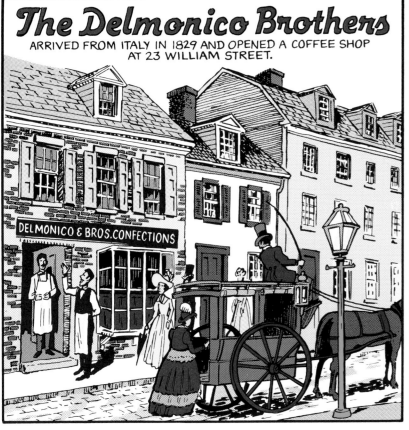

The Delmonico Brothers

ARRIVED FROM ITALY IN 1829 AND OPENED A COFFEE SHOP AT 23 WILLIAM STREET.

DELMONICO & BROS. CONFECTIONS

IN A SINGLE ROOM THEY & THEIR FAMILY MEMBERS MADE AND SOLD *BON BONS*, *PATÉS*, COFFEE, AND CONFECTIONS.

THEIR EXCELLENT FOOD AND COURTEOUS SERVICE WERE SO MUCH BETTER THAN THE OTHER EATERIES IN TOWN THAT SOON DELMONICO'S WAS INUNDATED WITH CUSTOMERS.

IN 1831 THEY OPENED A FULLY APPOINTED RESTAURANT AND IMPORTED A FRENCH CHEF WHO DAZZLED NEW YORKERS' PALATES WITH CAREFULLY PREPARED ENDIVE AND EGGPLANT.

TO GUARANTEE THE SUPPLY AND QUALITY OF INGREDIENTS ON THEIR MENU, THE DELMONICOS MAINTAINED THEIR OWN 200 ACRE FARM IN BROOKLYN.

James Monroe was a frequent visitor to New York. At 28, he married Elizabeth Kortright, daughter of a wealthy merchant at 56 Greenwich Street. In his private life Monroe was dominated by his wife and 2 daughters, Eliza and Maria, whom people regarded as notorious snobs. They went through his money so fast that he was in a financial bind when he died.

...DIED ON THE FOURTH OF JULY

THE 2nd AND 3rd PRESIDENTS OF THE U.S., JOHN ADAMS AND THOMAS JEFFERSON, DIED ON THE SAME DAY, JULY 4th, 1826, A HALF-CENTURY AFTER THEY BOTH SIGNED THE DECLARATION OF INDEPENDENCE.

FIVE YEARS LATER, ON JULY 4th, 1831, OUR 5th PRESIDENT, **JAMES MONROE**, DIED IN THE HOME OF HIS DAUGHTER, MRS. SAMUEL GOUVERNEUR AT 63 PRINCE ST., MANHATTAN.

NEW YORK HELD ONE OF ITS GRANDEST FUNERALS EVER, STARTING WITH A PRELIMINARY SERVICE AT CITY HALL, ATTENDED BY ALL THE MILITARY FORCES IN THE CITY.

THE STATE FUNERAL WAS CONDUCTED IN ST. PAUL'S CHAPEL BY THE RIGHT REV. BENJAMIN T. ONDERDONK, EPISCOPAL BISHOP OF NEW YORK.

HE WAS BURIED IN THE MARBLE CEMETERY AT 2nd AVE. BETWEEN 2nd AND 3rd STS.

THERE, PRES. MONROE RESTED IN PEACE FOR 27 YEARS UNTIL THE CITIZENS OF HIS NATIVE VIRGINIA WANTED HIM BACK.

THE CORPSE WAS DISINTERRED IN 1858, AND AGAIN LAY IN STATE IN CITY HALL, AND WAS GIVEN ANOTHER FUNERAL.

THE CASKET WAS PLACED ON THE S.S. JAMESTOWN WHICH LEFT NEW YORK HARBOR ON JULY 3rd, 1858. THE 7th N.Y. REG'T. CHARTERED THE S.S. ERICCSON TO ACCOMPANY THE JAMESTOWN TO VIRGINIA.

MONROE WAS LAID TO REST FOR THE LAST TIME IN THE HOLLY-WOOD CEMETERY IN RICHMOND, VIRGINIA.

There are streets named after President Monroe in the Bronx, Lower Manhattan, Brooklyn, Garden City, and Long Beach.

To build his ornamental garden at the "Stadium," Mr. Niblo transplanted large trees and employed several full-time gardners to tend the thousands of choice flowers and exotic plants. His guests sat amid this splendid flora and gushing fountains. Niblo's Garden was the first big-time theater in America.

The "Stadium"

During its sixty year lifespan, from 1834 to 1895, almost every famous entertainer appeared on its stage.

AT THE CORNER OF BROADWAY AND PRINCE STREET WAS A FIELD CALLED THE "STADIUM." THE NEW YORK MILITIA OFTEN USED IT AS A HORSE-TRAINING GROUND DURING THE WAR OF 1812.

LATER IT WAS OCCUPIED BY A CIRCUS. BY 1828 THIS AREA WAS STILL CONSIDERED SOMEWHAT REMOTE FROM NEW YORK CITY.

NEVERTHELESS, THE "STADIUM" WAS PURCHASED BY **WILLIAM NIBLO** WHO OPERATED THE BANK COFFEE SHOP AT PINE AND WILLIAM STREETS.

NIBLO CONVERTED THE CIRCUS BUILDING INTO A THEATER SURROUNDED BY GARDENS, TREES, WALKS, AND SUMMER HOUSES. BIG-TIME BROADWAY ENTERTAINMENT WAS ABOUT TO BEGIN WITH THE OPENING OF **NIBLO'S GARDEN** IN 1828.

The Ravels mentioned here were a famous French family of rope dancers, acrobats, and pantomimists. Consisting of ten persons, they originally came to the USA in 1832 and made their first appearance in the Park Theater.

NIBLO'S GARDEN

THE OPENING OF NIBLO'S GARDENS AT THE NORTHEAST CORNER OF BROADWAY AND PRINCE STREET ON JULY 4, 1828 WAS THE BEGINNING OF BIG-TIME ENTERTAINMENT IN NEW YORK.

FOR THE PRICE OF A NICKEL, CUSTOMERS WERE TREATED TO OUTDOOR THEATER AND A SCHOONER OF BEER. MR. NIBLO SOLD EXTRA SCHOONERS AT FIVE CENTS EACH.

ON RAINY DAYS AND DURING THE COLD WEATHER MONTHS, THE PATRONS MOVED INDOORS TO THE THEATER AT THE CENTER OF THE GARDEN. HERE, WILLIAM NIBLO STAGED PLAYS, OPERAS, AND MUSICAL REVUES WITH THE BIGGEST NAMES OF THE DAY, SUCH AS THE RAVELS, ADELINA PATTI, EDWIN FORREST, AND THE BOOTHS.

Places of entertainment were few and far between in the early 19th century. Consequently, John Scudder was able to draw a crowd at his American Museum with exhibits that included wax figures of heroes and villians, stuffed birds and reptiles, and his collection of live animals and freaks.

The Museum

JOHN PINTARD, A PROMINENT LAWYER, BUSINESSMAN, AND AUTHOR CONVINCED THE TAMMANY SOCIETY TO SPONSOR A MUSEUM DEDICATED TO AMERICAN HISTORY, ART, AND NATURE. THIS, THE FIRST MUSEUM IN NEW YORK, OPENED IN 1791 IN THE WEST WING OF THE ALMSHOUSE AT CITY HALL PARK.

GARDNER BAKER, ITS CURATOR, PURCHASED THE COLLECTION IN 1793. AFTER HIS DEATH, IN 1810, THE MUSEUM PIECES WERE SOLD TO **JOHN SCUDDER** WHO MOVED THEM TO 21 CHATHAM ST.

SCUDDER ADDED ODDITIES FROM VISITING SEA CAPTAINS. IN 1830 HE LEASED A NEW FIVE-STORY BUILDING AT BROADWAY & ANN ST.

AFTER SCUDDER DIED, HIS DAUGHTERS INHERITED HIS MUSEUM.

BUSINESS DECLINED, SO THE DAUGHTERS DECIDED TO SELL THE COLLECTION FOR $15,000.

CLOSED

IN 1841 AN ADVERTISING COPY-WRITER MADE A DEAL TO RENT THE BUILDING AND BUY THE COLLECTION FOR $12,000.

HIS NAME WAS PHINEAS TAYLOR **BARNUM.**

After successfully running Scudder's Museum, "Mr. Showmanship" opened a much bigger place uptown.

P.T. BARNUM OPENED HIS AMERICAN MUSEUM ON THE MORNING OF NEW YEAR'S DAY, 1842 IN A BUILDING THAT STRETCHED FROM ANN TO BEEKMAN STREET ALONG BROADWAY.

HORSECARS AND STAGECOACHES UNLOADED HUNDREDS OF POTENTIAL CUSTOMERS ALMOST AT HIS FRONT DOOR.

Barnum's Place

QUICKLY BECAME A TOP TOURIST ATTRACTION IN NEW YORK, VISITED BY THOUSANDS INCLUDING THE PRINCE OF WALES, CHARLES DICKENS, MARK TWAIN AND COLONEL GEORGE CUSTER.

ADMISSION TO HIS PART-MUSEUM AND PART-CARNIVAL SIDE-SHOW WAS 25¢. KIDS GOT IN FOR HALF-PRICE.

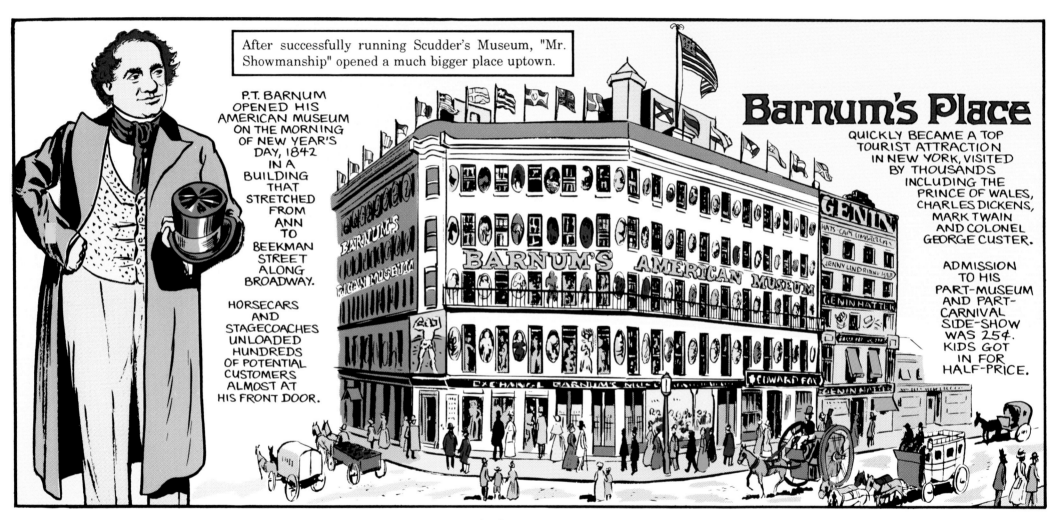

22

Beside the museum was a billiard parlor that had been converted into living quarters for Barnum's family who had to live on $600 a year until P. T. had paid off the loan for the museum.

Edgar Allan Poe arrived in New York on April 6, 1844 with his invalid wife and $4.50 in his pocket. They boarded for a while at 130 Greenwich St., then moved out to a farm at what is now 84th St. and Broadway. This is where he composed *The Raven* which brought him national fame, but very little money.

Poe in the Bronx

The Poes were so poor while living in the Bronx that they could not afford fuel, food, or clothing. Consequently, Virginia failed rapidly

EDGAR ALLAN POE AND HIS WIFE, VIRGINIA, MOVED FROM MANHATTAN TO THIS COTTAGE AT GRAND CONCOURSE & KINGSBRIDGE RD. IN THE BRONX IN JUNE, 1846. HE HOPED THE CLEAN COUNTRY AIR WOULD CURE VIRGINIA WHO WAS DYING OF TUBERCULOSIS.

POE WAS ALREADY FAMOUS FOR WRITING SUCH STORIES AS "THE MURDERS IN THE RUE MORGUE," "THE GOLD BUG," "THE PIT & THE PENDULUM," AND POEMS LIKE "THE RAVEN."

UNFORTUNATELY, MONEY DID NOT ACCOMPANY HIS FAME, AND THE RENT FOR THIS HOUSE, $100 PER YEAR, WAS CHEAPER THAN IN THE CITY.

AS POE STRUGGLED WITH HIS LITERARY CAREER, HIS MOTHER-IN-LAW, MARIA CLEMM, TOOK CARE OF HER DAUGHTER.

TO SUPPLEMENT HIS INCOME, POE OFTEN LECTURED NEARBY AT ST. JOHN'S COLLEGE, NOW FORDHAM UNIVERSITY.

MRS. POE COULD NOT SURVIVE THE WINTER. SHE DIED ON JAN. 30, 1847.

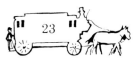

23

Poe met the women to whom he proposed during lecture tours. Sarah Helen Whitmore was a charming widow and a fine writer from Providence, Rhode Island. Opposition from her relatives squelched their wedding plans. The other was Ann Richmond of Lowell, Massachusetts. She had two reasons for not marrying Poe: he drank too much, and she was already married.

The Last Days of Poe

The city of New York took control of some land across the street from Poe's cottage in the Bronx and called it Poe Park. In 1913 the cottage was moved into the park for preservation.

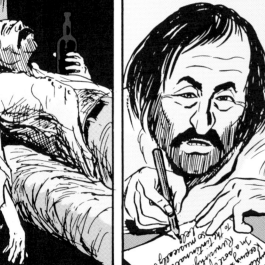

AFTER THE DEATH OF HIS WIFE, VIRGINIA, IN JANUARY, 1847, EDGAR ALLAN POE'S PROBLEMS WITH ALCOHOL AND DRUGS GREW WORSE, AS DID HIS HALLUCINATIONS AND PARANOIA.

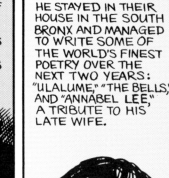

HE STAYED IN THEIR HOUSE IN THE SOUTH BRONX AND MANAGED TO WRITE SOME OF THE WORLD'S FINEST POETRY OVER THE NEXT TWO YEARS: "ULALUME," "THE BELLS," AND "ANNABEL LEE," A TRIBUTE TO HIS LATE WIFE.

TO ESCAPE GRIEF & LONELINESS, POE PURSUED WOMEN WITH A PASSION. IN 1848 TWO WOMEN REJECTED HIS PROPOSALS OF MARRIAGE.

THE FOLLOWING YEAR HE WENT TO RICHMOND, VA., WHERE HE GREW UP...

TO COURT HIS CHILDHOOD SWEETHEART, NOW A WIDOW.

HE PROPOSED TO MRS. SARAH ELMIRA ROYSTER SHELTON IN SEPTEMBER, 1849 AND SHE ACCEPTED.

I MUST RETURN TO NEW YORK TO TIE UP SOME BUSINESS BEFORE WE GET MARRIED.

HE BOARDED A STEAMBOAT TO BALTIMORE WHERE HE PLANNED TO CATCH A NORTHBOUND TRAIN.

ON OCT. 3, 1849 DR. JAMES E SNODGRASS FOUND POE UNCONSCIOUS IN A GUTTER ON LOMBARD ST., BALTIMORE.

MR. POE DIED FOUR DAYS LATER, PRESUMABLY OF ALCOHOLISM, BUT THE EXACT CAUSE WAS NEVER VERIFIED. HE WAS ONLY 40 YEARS OLD.

It is 13.9 miles long and 7.3 miles wide at its largest dimensions, and separated from Manhattan by Upper New York Bay, from Brooklyn by Lower New York Bay and the Narrows, and from New Jersey by Kill Van Kull and Arthur Kill. (Kill is Dutch for channel).

STATEN ISLAND

This is New York's third largest borough in area (60.9 square miles) and smallest in population (350,000+).

THE EXPLORER, HENRY HUDSON, GAVE THE BOROUGH ITS NAME, *STAATEN EYLANDT*, AFTER THE **STATES GENERAL**, THE POLITICIANS WHO RAN THE NETHERLANDS IN 1609.

THE BRITISH TOOK CONTROL OF NEW AMSTERDAM IN 1664 AND RENAMED THE ISLAND **RICHMOND** IN HONOR OF THE DUKE OF RICHMOND, THE ILLEGITIMATE SON OF KING CHARLES II.

THE BOROUGH'S FLAG WAS DESIGNED IN 1948 BY FERNAND O. FINGADO.

RICHMOND S N YORK 1683 1898 BOROUGH

MORE RECENTLY, THE FLAG BELOW IS CONSIDERED THE ISLAND'S COLORS. NEITHER FLAG WAS EVER *OFFICIAL*.

STATEN ISLAND

THIS MAP ROUGHLY SHOWS OVER 60 OF THE ISLAND'S VILLAGES.

Mr. Ward's cement house was so classy that, at one time, the English Consul General occupied the place as a summer home.

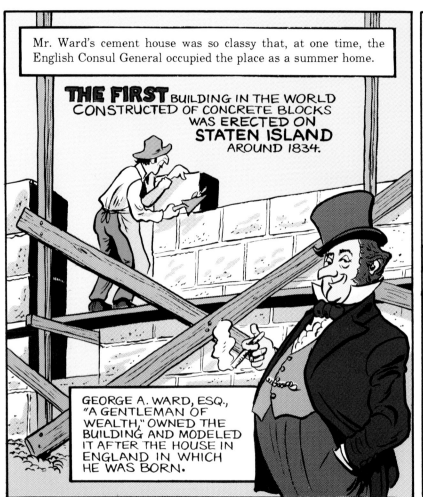

THE FIRST BUILDING IN THE WORLD CONSTRUCTED OF CONCRETE BLOCKS WAS ERECTED ON **STATEN ISLAND** AROUND 1834.

GEORGE A. WARD, ESQ., "A GENTLEMAN OF WEALTH," OWNED THE BUILDING AND MODELED IT AFTER THE HOUSE IN ENGLAND IN WHICH HE WAS BORN.

THE WARD HOUSE

THE HOUSE STOOD AT THE CORNER OF TERRACE AND FRANKLIN AVENUES IN NEW BRIGHTON. IT WAS SO UNIQUE THAT PEOPLE FROM ALL OVER THE WORLD CAME TO STATEN ISLAND TO SEE IT.

THE WARD HOUSE WAS DEMOLISHED IN 1920.

BUNS 1¢

Development of Staten Island's North and East Shores began shortly after the War of 1812 when large tracts of land were purchased by Daniel D. Tompkins for whom Tompkinsville was named. Governor of New York at the time, Tompkins was picked as James Monroe's running mate in 1816 and served two terms as Vice President of the United States. Tompkins's sister married Caleb T. Ward's father which accounts for Caleb's middle name - Tompkins.

MANY WEALTHY NEW YORK MERCHANTS BUILT IMPOSING MANSIONS ON STATEN ISLAND IN THE 1830'S, INCLUDING CALEB T. WARD OF WESTCHESTER. IN 1826 HE BEGAN ACQUIRING LAND IN THE STAPLETON SECTION OF THE ISLAND. BY 1835 HE HAD AN ESTATE OF 250 ACRES AND HIRED GEORGE B. DAVIS TO DESIGN A GREEK REVIVAL HOUSE CONSTRUCTED OF MARBLE.

The *Other* Ward Mansion

THE MANSION REMAINED IN THE WARD FAMILY UNTIL 1904 WHEN IT WAS SOLD TO SALLY NIXON. SHE SOLD IT IN 1923 AND IT WAS CONVERTED INTO APARTMENTS. A NEW OWNER RENOVATED IT DURING THE 1970'S. NOW A CITY LANDMARK, THE MANSION STANDS AT 141 NIXON AVENUE ON THE CREST OF STATEN ISLAND'S WARD HILL.

After building the first trolley car, John Stephenson enlarged his factory and went on to produce street cars for cities all over the world. In 1878, his cars cost between $1,000 and $1,200.

CLANG! CLANG!

All of the early street cars had names. Shown in the last panel is the John Mason, which honors the company's first vice-president. He took over the presidency in 1832 after Campbell P. Wright (who was also a Congressman) retired.

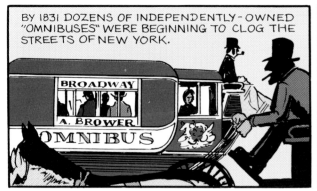

BY 1831 DOZENS OF INDEPENDENTLY-OWNED "OMNIBUSES" WERE BEGINNING TO CLOG THE STREETS OF NEW YORK.

MEANWHILE THE NEW *LOCOMOTIVE* CAUGHT THE ATTENTION OF A PROMINENT BANKER, MERCHANT, AND MAN-ABOUT-TOWN NAMED JOHN **MASON**.

EXPERIMENTAL LOCOMOTIVE RUNS IN HOBOKEN

I WANT TO BUILD A STREET RAILWAY!

HE WRANGLED A CHARTER FROM THE STATE LEGISLATURE.

State of New York Charter New York & Harlem R.R.

TRACKS WERE LAID FOR MR. MASON'S NEW YORK AND HARLEM RAILROAD FROM NEAR CITY HALL, UP 4th AVENUE TO 42nd STREET.

NEXT, MASON CONTRACTED WITH JOHN STEPHENSON, A MECHANIC ON 4th AVENUE, TO BUILD TWO HORSE-DRAWN RAIL CARS.

AMID MUCH HOOPLA, COMPANY OFFICIALS AND POLITICIANS MADE A TRIAL RUN IN NOVEMBER, 1832 ON THE **FIRST STREET-CAR LINE IN AMERICA**. TRAVEL IN THE FAST LANE HAD BEGUN.

28

The New York & Harlaem Railroad bought its first steam locomotive in 1837. The *George Washington*, shown in the first panel, was built by William Norris of Philadelphia in 1835 and initially ran on the Baltimore & Ohio line. The Harlaem's president from 1850 to 1853 was George L. Schuyler, descendant of a Revolutionary War hero.

Dawn of the Commuter Age

Mr. Schuyler was one of the most respected men in the state until he pulled off a $2 million stock swindle that nearly broke the company.

THE NEW YORK & HARLAEM RAILROAD WAS CHARTERED IN 1831 AS A HORSE-DRAWN TROLLEY LINE, BUT EVENTUALLY EXPANDED NORTHWARD. CONSTRUCTION BEGAN IN THE BRONX, AND ITS TRACKS REACHED FORDHAM IN 1841. STEPHEN JENKINS, HISTORIAN OF THE BRONX REMARKED, "THE GROWTH OF THE BRONX MAY BE DATED FROM 1842."

THE NY&H STRETCHED TO WHITE PLAINS IN 1845 AND VILLAGES IN WESTCHESTER COUNTY SPROUTED LIKE WEEDS. DAIRIES BEGAN TO SHIP MILK TO THE CITY DAILY, AND WITH FREQUENT SERVICE BETWEEN THE CITY AND THE COUNTRY, A NEW BREED OF AMERICAN EMERGED— **THE COMMUTER.**

IN 1853 A YEARLY FIRST-CLASS COMMUTER TICKET BETWEEN WHITE PLAINS AND NEW YORK CITY COST **$45.**

...AND IT WAS IN 1855 THAT ANOTHER INNOVATION FIRST APPEARED. A MAN NAMED MORGAN MAPES APPLIED TO THE NEW YORK & HARLAEM'S BOARD OF DIRECTORS FOR A CONTRACT TO PLACE **ADVERTISEMENTS** IN ITS CARS.

NOW APPEARING THE BOWERY THEATER Edwin Booth "Hamlet"

The New York & Harlaem Railroad hit hard times in the late 1850's. That's when Cornelius Vanderbilt made his move. He lent money to the company in 1857 and bought a large portion of the $1 million bond issue of 1858, much of it at 50 cents on the dollar. He was made a director of the company in 1858, but could see no future in the road and seldom attended board meetings. When the Civil War broke out, the Harlaem's stock rose from $3 a share to $12.

The Franchise Fracas

Vanderbilt soon realized that the future of America's transportation was in railroads, and he was determined to be a driving force in that industry.

THE EARLY RAIL-ROADS ENTERED AND LEFT NEW YORK ON FERRIES AND STEAMBOATS, MANY OF WHICH WERE OWNED BY "COMMODORE" **CORNELIUS VANDERBILT.** NATURALLY, HE OWNED STOCK IN SEVERAL RAILROADS.

BY 1862 HE WAS A DIRECTOR OF THE NEW YORK AND HARLAEM RAILROAD.

GENTLEMEN, HORSE-CAR LINES IN THE CITY ARE MORE PROFITABLE THAN OUR UP STATE LINES.

LET US *ENTICE* OUR CITY COUNCILMEN TO GRANT US A STREET CAR FRANCHISE ON BROADWAY FROM UNION SQUARE TO THE BATTERY.

MANY OF OUR CITY FATHERS RECEIVED "GIFTS" OF HARLAEM STOCKS AND BONDS.

IN APRIL, 1863, CITY COUNCIL GRANTED THE FRANCHISE.

HARLAEM'S STOCK HAS JUMPED FROM 60 TO 75 IN THE LAST HOUR!

MANY POLITICIANS GOT WEALTHIER AS MAYOR OPDYKE SIGNED THE FRANCHISE.

IMMEDIATELY WORKERS BEGAN TEARING UP THE BROADWAY PAVEMENT BELOW 14th STREET.

SIMULTANEOUSLY, A GROUP OF SPECULATORS HEADED BY ONE OF VANDERBILT'S ENEMIES, GEORGE LAW, WENT TO ALBANY AND...

BRIBED A FEW LEGISLATORS TO PASS A BILL THAT WOULD CANCEL THE HARLAEM'S FRANCHISE AND GIVE THE BROADWAY STREET CAR FRANCHISE TO MR. LAW'S GANG.

Introduced in the last panel is Daniel Drew (1797-1879). He settled in New York in 1829 and soon owned the principal stockyards in the city. Quick-witted and unscrupulous, he proved himself unmatched as a swindler.

IN 1863 GEORGE LAW BRIBED THE STATE LEGISLATURE TO PASS A BILL GIVING HIM A FRANCHISE TO RUN A STREET CAR LINE ON LOWER BROADWAY.

IMMEDIATELY HE WIRED HIS WORK GANGS TO START TEARING UP THE PAVEMENT ON BROADWAY SO THEY COULD LAY THE TRACKS.

NEXT, HE GOT AN INJUNCTION TO STOP THE NEW YORK AND HARLAEM FROM BUILDING THEIR LINE FARTHER UP BROADWAY.

AN UPROAR ERUPTED IN CITY HALL.

THE HARLAEM PLANS TO PAY THE CITY FOR ITS FRANCHISE...

TEN PERCENT OF ITS YEARLY GROSS, PLUS $25 PER CAR.

MR. LAW WILL GIVE THE CITY NOTHING!

PROMINENT CITIZENS SUCH AS SAMUEL J. TILDEN, WILLIAM B. ASTOR, AND PIERRE LORILLARD WIRED GOV. SEYMOUR PROTESTING MR. LAW'S FRANCHISE.

SEYMOUR, WHO SELDOM DID ANYTHING ON HIS OWN, FOLLOWED TILDEN'S ADVICE AND VETOED THE BILL FOR LAW'S FRANCHISE.

WHEN NEWS OF THE VETO REACHED WALL STREET, THE HARLAEM'S STOCK SHOT UP TO $100 PER SHARE.

IT WAS A VICTORY FOR CORNELIUS VANDERBILT, AND A SHORT TIME LATER HE WAS ELECTED PRESIDENT OF THE NY & HARLAEM RAILROAD.

MEANWHILE, ONE OF VANDERBILT'S WORST ENEMIES, "UNCLE DAN" DREW, WAS CONSPIRING WITH "BOSS" TWEED TO DERAIL THE NY & HARLAEM RAILROAD.

Cornelius Vanderbilt was one of the richest men in the world when he died in 1877 at the age of 83. His estate of some $104 million was $2 million more than the entire US Treasury at the time. About 90 percent of his fortune was made from railroads, although he hated railroads and refused to have anything to do with them until 15 years before he died.

Plot-Counterplot

The Broadway street car squabble spawned a new phrase on Wall Street during the 1860's, "Short of Harlaem," meaning any sort of bad luck.

WHEN VANDERBILT TOOK OVER THE NEW YORK AND HARLAEM RAILROAD IN THE SPRING OF 1863, DANIEL DREW, HIS OLD COMPETITOR IN THE STEAMBOAT BUSINESS, APPROACHED "BOSS" TWEED AND OTHER POLITICIANS WITH A DEVIOUS SCHEME.

REPEAL THE HARLAEM'S FRANCHISE TO BUILD A STREET CAR LINE ON BROADWAY.

THE HARLAEM'S STOCK WILL DROP WE'LL SELL SHORT AND MAKE A NICE **PROFIT!**

ON JUNE 25 THE STATE REPEALED THE HARLAEM'S STREET CAR FRANCHISE AND ITS STOCK FELL FROM 100 TO 73.

BUT THEIR PLOT BACKFIRED BECAUSE VANDERBILT AND HIS COHORTS STARTED TO **BUY** HARLAEM STOCK, DRIVING ITS PRICE TO 106.

THIS FORCED THE CROOKED POLITICIANS INTO **BANKRUPTCY.**

MARGIN CALL YOU OWE $50,000

VANDERBILT EXHULTED,

WE BUSTED THE WHOLE LEGISLATURE! SOME MEMBERS HAD TO GO HOME WITHOUT PAYING THEIR ROOM AND BOARD.

FACING A $1.2 MILLION LOSS, "UNCLE DAN" DREW WENT WHINING TO VANDERBILT.

AN OLD RIVER PAL OUGHT NOT BE HARD ON A FELLA THAT WAS JUST TRYIN' TO GET ALONG.

AFTER A FEW DAYS OF CONFERENCES, VANDERBILT STUCK DREW WITH A BILL OF **$1 MILLION.**

WHEN THE DUST SETTLED, THE HOPED-FOR STREET CAR LINE WHICH CAUSED ALL THE TROUBLE WAS SHELVED.

...IT'S TOO CONTROVERSIAL FOR THE TIMES.

During the first half of the 19th century, roller skating was limited to stage productions. German ballet masters used roller skates to simulate ice skating in the ballet *The Artist, or Winter Pleasures*. Giacomo Meyerbeer, a German composer, created an ice carnival scene in 1849 for his opera *Le Prophete*, which called for an entire ballet company on roller skates. It was a smash hit throughout Europe and America.

ROLLER SKATES

WERE INVENTED IN BELGIUM IN 1759 BY JOSEPH MERLIN, A MAKER OF MUSICAL INSTRUMENTS. HE PLANNED TO USE THEM TO MAKE A SPECTACULAR ENTRANCE AT A COSTUME BALL.

UNFORTUNATELY, HE NEVER LEARNED HOW TO STOP ON HIS SKATES. HE CRASHED INTO A MIRROR AND WAS SERIOUSLY INJURED.

THAT ENDED THE PUBLIC'S INTEREST IN ROLLER SKATING FOR A WHILE.

AROUND 1862 JAMES LEONARD **PLIMPTON,** A FURNITURE MAKER FROM MASSACHU-SETTS, MOVED TO NEW YORK.

HE BEGAN TO ICE-SKATE IN CENTRAL PARK FOR HIS HEALTH.

WHEN SPRING CAME, PLIMPTON WANTED TO CONTINUE HIS SKATING SO, IN 1863, HE PATENTED A PAIR OF WOODEN SKATES, EACH WITH FOUR WHEELS.

TO PROMOTE HIS INVENTION, PLIMPTON OPENED A FEW ROLLER-SKATING RINKS

BY 1870 ROLLER-SKATING WAS VERY POPULAR IN MOST OF THE U.S. AND OVER A DOZEN OTHER COUNTRIES.

MR. PLIMPTON BECAME A MILLIONAIRE, AND NO WONDER. IN AN ERA WHEN A DECENT SALARY WAS $1.00 A DAY, A PAIR OF HIS SKATES COST $20.

Christmas trees originated in Germany during the Middle Ages.

People put up trees in their homes and decorated them with candles to symbolize Christ as the Light of the World.

The Tree Bonanza

MARK CARR LIVED IN THE CATSKILLS AMONG GERMAN FARMERS DURING THE MID 19th CENTURY. IN DECEMBER, 1851 HE MADE A DEAL WITH SOME OF THEM TO BUY AND CHOP DOWN A FEW OX-SLEDS OF THEIR FIR TREES. THEN, HE LOADED THEM ON A STEAMBOAT AND SHIPPED THEM TO NEW YORK CITY.

MR. CARR SOLD THEM AT A HANDSOME PROFIT AT THE WASHINGTON MARKET, VESEY AND FULTON STREETS. THUS BEGAN THE COMMERCIAL CHRISTMAS TREE INDUSTRY.

Harper's Weekly was the largest illustrated newspaper in the United States when Thomas Nast joined its art staff in 1861.

Nast, however, hated working in the art room among dozens of other artists. But his talent was so great that the publisher, Fletcher Harper, allowed the young artist to work at home.

The Jolly Ol' Elf

SANTA CLAUS HAS BEEN AROUND FOR CENTURIES, BUT IT WAS NOT UNTIL THE CIVIL WAR THAT HE BEGAN TO LOOK THE WAY HE DOES TODAY, THANKS TO A CARTOONIST WHO LIVED AT 5th AVE. & 125th ST. ~ **THOMAS NAST.**

FROM 1863 TO 1886, NAST CREATED A SERIES OF CHRISTMAS DRAWINGS FOR *HARPER'S WEEKLY* IN WHICH SANTA EVOLVED FROM A PUDGY ELF TO THE FULL-SIZE, BEARDED, POT-BELLIED CHARACTER SEEN IN STORES AND MALLS ACROSS THE WORLD TODAY.

MR. NAST CONTRIBUTED TO THE SANTA LORE BY SHOWING HOW HE SPENT HIS ENTIRE YEAR-MAKING TOYS IN HIS NORTH POLE WORKSHOP, CHECKING ON CHILDREN'S BEHAVIOR, KEEPING A LIST OF WHO'S NAUGHTY AND NICE, AND READING THEIR LISTS OF CHRISTMAS WISHES.

Over the years New York's mayors have been called many things, but Fernando Wood was blasted with such epithets as *traitor*, *blackguard*, and *fool*. Here's why...

THE CITY-STATE OF TRIINSULA

WHEN ABE LINCOLN WAS ELECTED PRESIDENT IN NOVEMBER, 1860 SOUTHERN STATES BEGAN TO SECEDE FROM THE UNION, SETTING THE STAGE FOR THE **CIVIL WAR.**

STATES' RIGHTS...

ON JANUARY 7, 1861, FERNANDO WOOD, MAYOR OF NEW YORK, SENT A SUPRISING MESSAGE TO THE CITY COUNCIL.

I RECOMMEND THAT NEW YORK CITY SECEDE FROM THE UNION AND BECOME A **FREE CITY.**

THE FEDERAL UNION IS FALLING APART AND WE CAN'T AFFORD TO JEOPARDIZE OUR PROFITABLE TRADE WITH THE SOUTH.

WE CAN KEEP THE FEDERAL GOVERNMENT FROM COLLECTING ALL THE RICH CUSTOM DUTIES POURING INTO THE CITY.

"WE WILL ANNEX STATEN ISLAND AND BROOKLYN AND CALL OURSELVES **TRIINSULA!**"

ISLAND

NOBODY TOOK MAYOR WOOD SERIOUSLY, BUT HE HAD THE LAST WORD. ON THE DAY LINCOLN WAS INAUGURATED, HE REFUSED TO LET THE FLAG FLY OVER CITY HALL.

After the 22nd Regiment was formed it became part of the New York State Militia on September 17, 1861. Not only did its members purchase their own uniforms, they also bought their own weapons - Enfield rifles from England.

Also called the *Strawberry Grays,* the 22nd originally tried to get gray fatigue jackets, but the manufacturer could not supply them, so they settled for blue. Their pants and hats were gray.

THE MONEY REGIMENT

AT THE OUTBREAK OF THE CIVIL WAR, NEW YORK CITY'S MILITIA UNITS ALL LEFT FOR WASHINGTON. CONCERNS OVER THE CITY'S SECURITY LED SOME **INSURANCE AND BANKING FIRMS** TO PUT UP THE MONEY TO FIELD SIX INFANTRY COMPANIES. ON MAY 13, 1861 THEY ORGANIZED THE **22nd REGIMENT.**

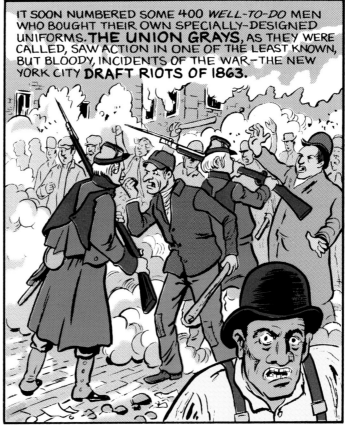

IT SOON NUMBERED SOME 400 *WELL-TO-DO* MEN WHO BOUGHT THEIR OWN SPECIALLY-DESIGNED UNIFORMS. **THE UNION GRAYS,** AS THEY WERE CALLED, SAW ACTION IN ONE OF THE LEAST KNOWN, BUT BLOODY, INCIDENTS OF THE WAR—THE NEW YORK CITY **DRAFT RIOTS OF 1863.**

THE ARMY MADE THEM **COMBAT ENGINEERS** IN 1902 AND THEY FOUGHT PANCHO VILLA'S GUERILLAS IN MEXICO IN 1916. DESIGNATED THE **102nd ENGINEERS** IN 1917, THEY SERVED IN BOTH WORLD WARS.

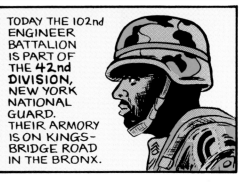

TODAY THE 102nd ENGINEER BATTALION IS PART OF THE **42nd DIVISION,** NEW YORK NATIONAL GUARD. THEIR ARMORY IS ON KINGS-BRIDGE ROAD IN THE BRONX.

When the Civil War started, the Union Army had only 115 doctors. Of these, 27 left the Army and returned to their homes in the South. By the end of the war, over 13,000 doctors had served in the Union forces.

The Confederate Surgeon

The Confederate Army had only 3,500 doctors. This is the story of one of them.

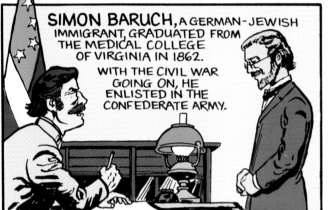

SIMON BARUCH, A GERMAN-JEWISH IMMIGRANT, GRADUATED FROM THE MEDICAL COLLEGE OF VIRGINIA IN 1862.

WITH THE CIVIL WAR GOING ON, HE ENLISTED IN THE CONFEDERATE ARMY.

HE WAS COMMISSIONED A CAPTAIN AND ASSIGNED AS A FIELD SURGEON.

FOLLOWING THE WAR, DR. BARUCH PRACTICED MEDICINE IN SOUTH CAROLINA UNTIL HE MOVED TO NEW YORK CITY IN 1881.

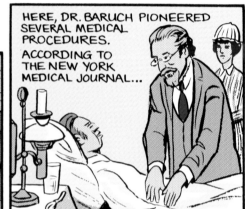

HERE, DR. BARUCH PIONEERED SEVERAL MEDICAL PROCEDURES.

ACCORDING TO THE NEW YORK MEDICAL JOURNAL...

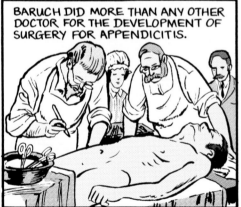

BARUCH DID MORE THAN ANY OTHER DOCTOR FOR THE DEVELOPMENT OF SURGERY FOR APPENDICITIS.

HE ALSO INTRODUCED HYDROTHERAPY TO THE U.S. — TREATING AILMENTS WITH WATER.

FROM HIS HOME AT 51 W. 70th ST., DR. BARUCH CRUSADED FOR IMPROVED HYGIENE AND SANITATION IN NEW YORK. IN 1901...

HE CONVINCED THE STATE LEGISLATURE TO SET UP FREE PUBLIC BATHS (THE COUNTRY'S FIRST) FOR TENEMENT DWELLERS.

SIMON BARUCH DIED IN 1921 AT AGE 80. BARUCH PLACE AND BARUCH DRIVE IN MANHATTAN WERE NAMED AFTER HIM, NOT HIS SON (SHOWN HERE), THE FINANCIER & PRESIDENTIAL ADVISOR, BERNARD BARUCH.

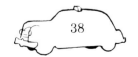

The Statue of Freedom, as it is officially known, faces East. As a protection from lightning, ten bronze points tipped with platinum were placed on the statue: one on the head, six on the feathers in the headdress, one on each shoulder, and one on the shield.

AT NOON, DECEMBER 2, 1863, EVERY GUN IN THE TWELVE FORTS AROUND WASHINGTON, D.C. FIRED A SALUTE.

THE GRAND OCCASION WAS THE RAISING OF THE HEAD SECTION OF A STATUE 287 FEET TO THE TOP OF THE RECENTLY COMPLETED CAPITOL DOME.

WHEN IT WAS BOLTED TO ITS SHOULDERS, THE STATUE OF FREEDOM STOOD 19½ FT. HIGH AND WEIGHED SEVEN TONS.

VIRTUALLY FORGOTTEN IS THE DESIGNER OF THIS MONUMENT, AMERICA'S FIRST GREAT SCULPTOR, **THOMAS CRAWFORD** OF NEW YORK CITY.

One of the earliest American sculptors was John Frazee. Born in 1790 in Rahway, NJ, he apprenticed to a bricklayer, but soon displayed a talent as a stone carver.

He moved to Greenwich Village and later founded the National Academy of Design. In 1831, he teamed up with Robert E. Launitz, a Latvian-born sculptor who studied with the great Thorvaldsen in Rome before moving to New York City.

THE ASPIRING SCULPTOR

Frazee and Launitz were teachers at the National Academy where they had a student who showed great promise. This is that student's story.

THOMAS CRAWFORD WAS BORN ON MARCH 22, 1813 IN MANHATTAN, THE SON OF IRISH IMMIGRANTS. BEFORE HE WAS TEN, THOMAS WAS DRAWING, PAINTING, AND CARVING FIGURES IN WOOD WITH A PEN KNIFE.

BUT IT WAS THE SIGHT OF STONE CUTTERS WORKING ON THE FACADES OF NEW BUILDINGS IN THE CITY THAT CONVINCED YOUNG CRAWFORD TO BECOME A SCULPTOR.

AT 19 HE ATTENDED THE NATIONAL ACADEMY OF DESIGN AT 23rd STREET AND 4th AVENUE. HE ALSO APPRENTICED AS A STONE CUTTER FOR JOHN FRAZEE AND ROBERT LAUNITZ.

FIGURING HE'D LEARN MORE IN EUROPE, THOMAS WENT TO ROME IN 1834 AT AGE 21, AND GOT A JOB COPYING STATUES FOR THE FAMOUS DANISH SCULPTOR ALBERT THORVALDSEN. THE PAY WAS LOUSY.

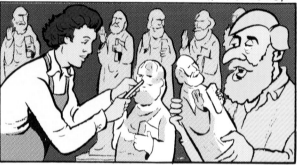

CRAWFORD LIVED IN POVERTY. NEVERTHELESS, HE KNOCKED OUT DOZENS OF STATUES IN HIS TINY APARTMENT WITHOUT EVER USING A MODEL.

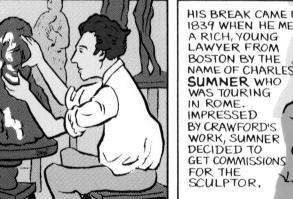

HIS BREAK CAME IN 1839 WHEN HE MET A RICH, YOUNG LAWYER FROM BOSTON BY THE NAME OF CHARLES SUMNER WHO WAS TOURING IN ROME. IMPRESSED BY CRAWFORD'S WORK, SUMNER DECIDED TO GET COMMISSIONS FOR THE SCULPTOR.

Crawford worked for Thorvaldsen for about a year. When the master left Rome, the young American was on his own. Commissions for unknown and untried sculptors were scarce, but a few came his way in 1836. Crawford was such a workaholic that he went on a ten week work binge in 1837, knocking out no less than seventeen portrait busts.

Friends in High Places

Despite all the work he turned out betweem 1836 and 1843, Crawford did not make much money.

THOMAS CRAWFORD WAS A NEW YORKER STRUGGLING TO MAKE IT AS A SCULPTOR IN ITALY. IN 1839 HIS FRIEND CHARLES SUMNER, OBTAINED A COMMISSION FOR CRAWFORD TO CREATE A STATUE OF *ORPHEUS* FOR THE BOSTON ATHENAEUM. THE ART CRITICS LOVED IT.

SOON THOMAS BECAME A CELEBRATED SCULPTOR WITH DOZENS OF COMMISSIONS.

EARLY IN 1843, LOUISA WARD, A DAUGHTER OF NEW YORK BANKERS, WAS IN ROME VISITING HER SISTER AND BROTHER-IN-LAW, JULIA WARD HOWE AND DR. SAM HOWE. THE HOWES KNEW CRAWFORD AND INTRODUCED HIM TO LOUISA. THEY FELL IN LOVE.

THOMAS FOLLOWED LOUISA TO NEW YORK WHERE THEY GOT MARRIED. IN 1846 THEY SETTLED IN ROME.

MEANWHILE, SUMNER WAS ELECTED TO THE U.S. SENATE FROM MASSACHUSETTS. THE CAPITOL WAS BEING RENOVATED IN 1851, AND SECRETARY OF WAR JEFFERSON DAVIS WAS IN CHARGE. SUMNER SUGGESTED HE USE CRAWFORD'S SERVICES.

THIS LED TO A $3,000 CONTRACT TO DESIGN THE *STATUE OF FREEDOM* FOR THE DOME IN 1854.

HIS FIRST SKETCHES OF THE FIGURE CAUSED SECRETARY OF WAR DAVIS TO BLOW HIS TOP.

While Crawford was designing the *Statue of Freedom*, he went to Munich, Germany to work with Ferdinand von Muller on other pieces. These included a marble carving of *Adam and Eve* for the Boston Athenaeum and a ten-foot high statue of James Otis for Mount Auburn Cemetery. The majestic marble *Otis* is now at Harvard University.

 # Jeff Davis and the Lady's Hat

THOMAS CRAWFORD DREW SOME SKETCHES OF THE *STATUE OF FREEDOM* IN HIS STUDIO IN ROME. IN JULY, 1855 HE SENT THEM TO SECRETARY OF WAR JEFFERSON DAVIS FOR APPROVAL. INSTEAD, DAVIS HAD A FIT.

WHAT *IS* THIS?!

THAT CARVER FROM NEW YORK AND HIS FRIEND, SENATOR SUMNER, ARE TRYIN' T' PULL AN ABOLITIONIST PLOT!

THAT HAT USED T' BE WORN BY FREED SLAVES IN ANCIENT ROME. TELL CRAWFORD T' GET RID OF IT!

CRAWFORD GOT THE MESSAGE. THAT IS WHY THE STATUE ON THE CAPITOL DOME SPORTS A HELMET RINGED BY STARS AND TOPPED WITH A BALD EAGLE.

The New York Historical Society on Central Park West has some sculptures which Crawford created in Rome during his "starvation" period which ran from 1836 to 1843.

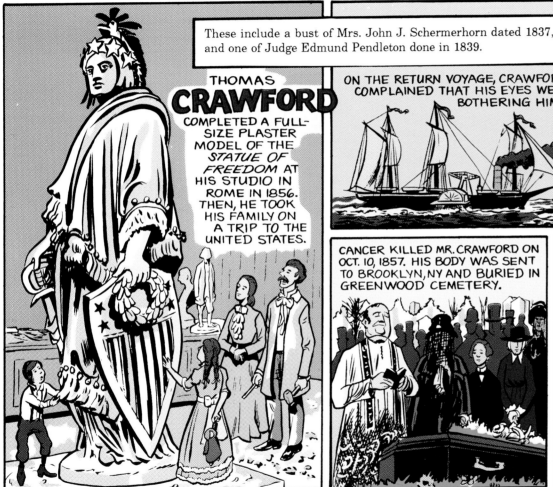

These include a bust of Mrs. John J. Schermerhorn dated 1837, and one of Judge Edmund Pendleton done in 1839.

THOMAS **CRAWFORD** COMPLETED A FULL-SIZE PLASTER MODEL OF THE *STATUE OF FREEDOM* AT HIS STUDIO IN ROME IN 1856. THEN, HE TOOK HIS FAMILY ON A TRIP TO THE UNITED STATES.

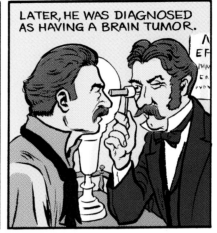

ON THE RETURN VOYAGE, CRAWFORD COMPLAINED THAT HIS EYES WERE BOTHERING HIM.

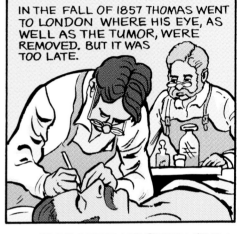

LATER, HE WAS DIAGNOSED AS HAVING A BRAIN TUMOR.

IN THE FALL OF 1857 THOMAS WENT TO LONDON WHERE HIS EYE, AS WELL AS THE TUMOR, WERE REMOVED. BUT IT WAS TOO LATE.

CANCER KILLED MR. CRAWFORD ON OCT. 10, 1857. HIS BODY WAS SENT TO BROOKLYN, NY AND BURIED IN GREENWOOD CEMETERY.

AROUND 1862, LOUISA CRAWFORD GAVE 87 PIECES OF HER HUSBAND'S WORK TO THE CITY OF NEW YORK. MANY ARE NOW AT THE METROPOLITAN MUSEUM OF ART AND THE NEW YORK HISTORICAL SOCIETY.

SIX YEARS AFTER HIS DEATH, CRAWFORD'S *STATUE OF FREEDOM* WAS FINALLY BOLTED TO THE TOP OF THE CAPITOL DOME IN WASHINGTON, D.C. BY A RECENTLY FREED SLAVE.

Colonel Johannes Hardenbergh used slaves to work his vast farm in Ulster County, New York. It was in the muddy slave cellar of the farmhouse that, around 1797, Mau-Mau Bett gave birth to a girl she named Isabella. In 1806 Isabella was sold at auction to John Nealy of Ulster County for the paltry sum of $100 and, allegedly, some sheep. Nealy sold her to Martin Scriver who in turn sold her to John Dumont.

FROM SLAVE TO EVANGELIST

THE ONLY NORTHERN STATES THAT PERMITTED SLAVERY AFTER THE REVOLUTIONARY WAR WERE NEW YORK AND NEW JERSEY. THE STATE OF NEW YORK PASSED A LAW TO ABOLISH SLAVERY AS OF JULY 4, 1827.

A YEAR EARLIER, JOHN DUMONT OF NEW PALZ, NEW YORK, HAD PROMISED FREEDOM FOR ONE OF HIS SLAVES, A 29 YEAR OLD WOMAN NAMED ISABELLA.

WHEN DUMONT FAILED TO KEEP HIS WORD, ISABELLA TOOK HER BABY DAUGHTER, THE ONLY ONE OF HER FIVE CHILDREN NOT TO HAVE BEEN SOLD AWAY FROM HER, AND SIMPLY WALKED OFF IN SEARCH OF HER FREEDOM.

EVENTUALLY SHE MOVED TO NEW YORK CITY AND WORKED FOR A MR. AND MRS. WHITING ON CANAL STREET.

ONE DAY IN 1843, ISABELLA RECEIVED "A DIVINE MESSAGE..."

Take to the road and spread the truth about the Lord

ON JUNE 1, 1843 THIS 46 YEAR OLD WOMAN CHANGED HER NAME, LEFT MANHATTAN, AND BEGAN HER EVANGELISTIC CRUSADE. AT FIRST SHE PREACHED AT CAMP MEETINGS ON LONG ISLAND.

TRAVELING ACROSS THE COUNTRY, SHE MET ABOLITIONISTS AND ADOPTED THEIR CAUSE.

THOUGH ILLITERATE, SHE COULD QUOTE SCRIPTURES & ELECTRIFY ANY AUDIENCE. TO EMPHASIZE HER SPIRITUAL GOAL IN LIFE, ISABELLA HAD TAKEN THE NAME SOJOURNER TRUTH.

When Isabella left Dumont's farm, she found refuge in the home of Mr. and Mrs. Isaac Van Wagener, a Quaker family. Naturally, Dumont came after Isabella but the Wageners purchased her from Dumont, then granted Isabella her freedom. From that day in 1826 until 1843, she went by the name of Isabella Van Wagener.

Sojourner Truth had a son named Peter who, at the age of four, was sold to a plantation owner in Alabama. At the time, it was illegal to sell a slave out of New York state. A year later she was granted her freedom and she immediately sued for the return of her son. She won and was soon reunited with Peter. She took him to New York City, but as he grew older he ran with the wrong crowd and was constantly in trouble..

"I am a New Yorker!"

When Peter was about 17 years old, Sojourner arranged for him to get a job aboard a whaling ship. She never saw him again. He wrote to her for a few years but then his letters stopped.

UPON LEAVING NEW YORK CITY IN 1843, SOJOURNER TRUTH TRAVELED ACROSS THE COUNTRY, GIVING ROUSING SPEECHES FOR WOMEN'S RIGHTS AND THE ABOLITION OF SLAVERY.

AFTER THE CIVIL WAR, SOJOURNER WAS IN WASHINGTON, D.C. HELPING THE NEWLY FREED SLAVES. ONE DAY IN 1865 SHE WAS TAKING CANDY AND BOOKS TO PATIENTS AT FREEDMANS' HOSPITAL. SEGREGATION ON STREETCARS IN THE CAPITAL HAD BEEN OUTLAWED, BUT NO DRIVER WOULD STOP FOR THE 68 YEAR OLD WOMAN.

FINALLY SHE GOT FED UP WITH BEING IGNORED AND STARTED YELLING...

I WANT TO RIDE!

HER BOOMING VOICE STOPPED TRAFFIC AND BLOCKED THE TRACKS. BEFORE THE STREETCAR COULD MOVE, SHE HOPPED ABOARD.

THE ENRAGED DRIVER TOLD HER TO STAND UP FRONT SO HE COULD THROW HER OFF.

I AM NOT A VIRGINIAN OR A MARYLANDER TO TREMBLE AT YOUR BULLYING. I AM A NEW YORKER AND I KNOW THE LAW!

I WILL SIT WITH THE OTHER PASSENGERS.

SOJOURNER STAYED ON THE TROLLEY AND A SHORT TIME LATER WASHINGTON'S STREETCAR DRIVERS BEGAN TO STOP FOR EVERYBODY.

THUS, A NEW YORKER WAS THE FIRST FREEDOM RIDER.

The Centre Street Shot Tower was constructed for the McCullogh Lead Company. Buckshot pellets were made here by splashing molten lead through screens at the top of the tower. The droplets then cooled into spheres as they fell through the air.

THE FLASHERS

The tower was built similar to a modern skyscraper - a framework of iron pillars filled in with bricks and mortar.

IN THE LAST HALF OF THE 19th CENTURY, ONE OF THE TALLEST STRUCTURES IN LOWER MANHATTAN WAS THE SHOT TOWER AT READE AND CENTRE STREETS. IT WAS BUILT IN THE 1850's BY JAMES BOGARDUS FOR THE MANUFACTURE OF GUNSHOT. THE GALLOWS IN THE TOMBS PRISON COULD BE SEEN FROM THE TOP OF THE TOWER.

WHENEVER A HANGING WAS SCHEDULED, REPORTERS GATHERED ATOP THE TOWER. AS SOON AS THE HANGMAN DROPPED THE TRAP DOOR,

THE NEWSMEN AIMED THEIR SIGNAL DEVICES TOWARD THEIR OFFICES AND *FLASHED* THE NEWS.

FROM THIS CAME THE TERM **NEWS FLASH!**

THE SHOT TOWER WAS KNOCKED DOWN IN 1908 TO MAKE WAY FOR THE IRT SUBWAY.

George Hartford's store (in the second panel) was gaily decorated in an Asian motif. Japanese lanterns hung from the ceiling and the cashier's cage resembled a Chinese pagoda.

A giant leap toward becoming a national chain came in 1871 when Mr. Hartford sent a trainload of coffee and tea to victims of the Chicago fire. He also set up a temporary store amid the ruins.

THE TEA MERCHANT

Later, Mr. Hartford built a permanent store in the Windy City. By 1880 he had 95 stores from Boston to Milwaukee.

GEORGE HUNTINGTON HARTFORD WAS 26 YEARS OLD WHEN, IN 1859, HE BOUGHT A SHIPLOAD OF TEA DIRECT FROM CHINA AND SOLD IT ON A DOCK IN NEW YORK FOR ABOUT A THIRD OF THE GOING PRICE IN THE CITY.

BY SKIPPING THE USUAL MIDDLEMEN, HARTFORD EARNED A NICE PROFIT. HE OPENED A STORE ON VESEY ST., AND HIRED A BAND TO DRUM UP BUSINESS ON SATURDAYS.

AS HARTFORD'S BUSINESS INCREASED, HE OPENED MORE STORES IN NEW YORK CITY. NEXT, HE EXPANDED WESTWARD, ADDING COFFEE AND SPICES TO HIS LINE.

MR. HARTFORD ALSO PUT A FLEET OF WAGONS ON THE ROAD SELLING HOUSE TO HOUSE. MANY DRIVERS LEARNED MERCHANDISING THIS WAY BEFORE MOVING UP TO TOP JOBS IN THE COMPANY.

IN 1871 HARTFORD CHANGED HIS CORPORATION'S NAME TO *THE ATLANTIC AND PACIFIC TEA COMPANY*, AND THAT WAS THE BEGINNING OF THE FIRST GROCERY STORE CHAIN - THE A & P.

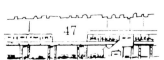

While attending school in Ireland, John Hughes became interested in the priesthood. In 1816, John's father and older brother immigrated to the U.S., sending for John the following year, and for the rest of the family in 1818.

"Digger" John Hughes

Although highly successful as a church pastor, Father John Hughes attracted more attention with his controversial writings and speeches.

AT THE AGE OF 20, IN 1817, JOHN J. HUGHES LEFT COUNTY TYRONE, **IRELAND** TO JOIN HIS FAMILY IN CHAMBERSBURG, PA.

HE WORKED IN A QUARRY WHILE TRYING TO ENROLL IN MOUNT ST. MARY'S SEMINARY AT EMMITSBURG, MARYLAND.

EVENTUALLY JOHN WAS HIRED AS A GARDENER AT MOUNT ST. MARY'S UNTIL A VACANCY OCCURRED.

THE YOUNG SEMINARIANS GAVE HIM A NICKNAME THAT WOULD STICK FOR THE REST OF HIS LIFE.

"DIGGER" JOHN

"DIGGER" WAS ORDAINED A PRIEST AT ST. JOSEPH'S CHURCH, PHILADELPHIA IN 1826. HE WAS 29.

ANTI-CATHOLICISM WAS RAMPANT AT THE TIME, AND FATHER HUGHES GAINED FAME FOR HIS CONTROVERSIAL WRITINGS AND SPEECHES DEFENDING CATHOLICS.

HE ESTABLISHED A CATHOLIC TRACT SOCIETY TO **DISTRIBUTE** FREE PAMPHLETS AND HE STARTED A NEWSPAPER.

The Catholic Herald

HIS ACHIEVEMENTS ATTRACTED THE ATTENTION OF THE CHURCH HIERARCHY, RESULTING IN PROMOTIONS.

THEN, IN 1837, POPE GREGORY XVI SENT FATHER HUGHES TO NEW YORK CITY. ON JAN. 7, 1838 "DIGGER" JOHN HUGHES WAS CONSECRATED AS **BISHOP OF NEW YORK** IN THE OLD **ST. PATRICK'S CATHEDRAL** AT MOTT AND PRINCE STREETS.

Chester Alan Arthur was born October 6, 1830 somewhere in Vermont. Two towns claim to have been his birthplace, but his political opponents said he was actually born across the border in Canada. If that were true, Mr. Arthur would have been ineligible to run for President or Vice-President of the United States.

Chester Alan Arthur

Mr. Arthur graduated Phi Beta Kappa from Union College in Schenectady, NY in 1848. He taught school until he moved to New York City in 1853 to work in the law office of a friend.

THE YEAR 1859 WAS AN EVENTFUL ONE FOR A 29 YEAR-OLD LAWYER IN NEW YORK NAMED CHESTER ALAN ARTHUR. HE JOINED THE STATE MILITIA, ENTERED POLITICS, AND MARRIED THE SOCIALLY PROMINENT ELLEN LEWIS HERNDON. THEY MOVED INTO HIS BRIDE'S HOME AT 34 WEST 21ST STREET.

THE FOLLOWING YEAR HE WORKED FOR THE RE-ELECTION OF EDWIN D. MORGAN AS GOVERNOR OF NEW YORK. IN RETURN, GOV. MORGAN PROMOTED ARTHUR TO ENGINEER-IN-CHIEF.

A FEW MONTHS LATER, THE CIVIL WAR BROKE OUT AND IT WAS GENERAL ARTHUR'S RESPONSIBILITY TO FEED, HOUSE, AND EQUIP THOUSANDS OF WAR-BOUND SOLDIERS POURING INTO NEW YORK FROM ALL OVER THE NORTH EAST.

THIS WAS THE MILITARY WARE-HOUSE AT 51 WALKER ST.

IN 1863, ARTHUR'S PATRON, EDWIN MORGAN, WAS ELECTED TO THE U.S. SENATE FROM NEW YORK.

MEANWHILE, ARTHUR RESIGNED AND WENT BACK TO PRACTICING LAW. ONE OF HIS CLIENTS WAS AN UNSCRUPULOUS HATTER BY THE NAME OF THOMAS MURPHY.

MURPHY WAS ACCUSED OF SELLING FAULTY HATS AND CAPS TO THE UNION ARMY DURING THE WAR.

THE CASE WENT BEFORE A SPECIAL COMMITTEE CHAIRED BY SENATOR MORGAN. NEEDLESS TO SAY, MURPHY GOT OFF LIGHTLY, AND HE AND ARTHUR BECAME CLOSE FRIENDS.

The New York Customhouse had jurisdiction over the sea waters and shores of New York state and most of Hudson and Bergen Counties in New Jersey. Its primary duties were to receive and record documents pertaining to the entry of ships, collect duties, and enforce the neutrality laws. By 1872 the Customhouse payroll was $1,800,000 per year. The Collector's salary was over $50,000 per annum.

THE CUSTOMS COLLECTOR

THERE WAS NO *CIVIL SERVICE* BY 1870. GOVERNMENT EMPLOYEES WERE HIRED AS PAYMENT FOR THEIR SERVICES TO THE WINNING POLITICAL PARTY.

IN RETURN, THESE EMPLOYEES HAD TO KICK BACK PART OF THEIR SALARIES TO THE PARTY TREASURY, AS WELL AS PERFORM REGULAR PARTY DUTIES.

THE RICHEST SOURCE OF POLITICALLY APPOINTED JOBS IN THE U.S. WAS THE CUSTOM HOUSE OF THE PORT OF NEW YORK. IT EMPLOYED OVER ONE THOUSAND PEOPLE.

IN 1870 PRESIDENT GRANT APPOINTED TOM MURPHY, A WEALTHY, SHIFTY HATTER, AS COLLECTOR OF CUSTOMS IN NEW YORK. MURPHY NOW HAD CONTROL OF ALL THE CUSTOM HOUSE JOBS.

WITHIN A YEAR, MURPHY WAS ACCUSED OF CORRUPTION AND FIRED.

SURPRISINGLY, THE PRESIDENT LET MURPHY NAME HIS REPLACEMENT.

I CHOOSE MY CLOSE FRIEND, CHESTER A. ARTHUR.

CHET ARTHUR'S INTEGRITY AND HARD WORK AS COLLECTOR OF CUSTOMS LED TO HIS NOMINATION AS VICE-PRESIDENT OF THE UNITED STATES IN 1880.

LATER, AS PRESIDENT, ARTHUR WOULD FIGHT POLITICAL PATRONAGE BY GETTING CONGRESS TO ENACT THE CIVIL SERVICE LAW OF 1883.

MURPHY WENT BANKRUPT. PRESIDENT ARTHUR NEVER GAVE HIM A JOB, NOR DID HE EVER INVITE HIS OLD FRIEND TO DINNER AT THE WHITE HOUSE.

The first known formally-educated veterinarian in New York was John Rose, a Prussian who arrived in the city around 1827. Twenty-nine years later, graduate veterinarians from Europe, especially from England, were settling in New York State. Among these were alumni of London's Royal College of Veterinary Surgeons who set up their practices in Manhattan: A. Lockhart, R. H. Curtis, and R. H. Budd.

Open wide and say "Neigh."

UNTIL THE LATTER PART OF THE 19th CENTURY, ANYONE WITH A KNACK FOR TREATING SICK OR INJURED ANIMALS COULD CALL THEMSELVES A **VETERINARIAN.**

THEIR METHODS WERE USUALLY HARSH AND INHUMANE.

JAMES CARVER OF PHILADELPHIA, PA. WENT TO ENGLAND AT THE AGE OF 40 TO STUDY AT THE LONDON VETERINARY COLLEGE. GRADUATING IN 1815 HE BECAME THE FIRST KNOWN AMERICAN TO EARN A VETERINARY DEGREE.

ON RETURNING TO THE U.S. HE SET UP HIS VETERINARY PRACTICE ON LONG ISLAND.

AN ATTEMPT WAS MADE IN 1810 TO ESTABLISH A VETERINARY SCHOOL IN NEW YORK, BUT SUCH AN EFFORT WOULD NOT BE SUCCESSFUL UNTIL 1857, THAT IS WHEN DR. JOHN BUSTEED STARTED THE NEW YORK COLLEGE OF VETERINARY SURGEONS AT 23rd STREET NEAR SIXTH AVENUE. IT WAS THE **FIRST** IN THE UNITED STATES.

THE COLLEGE WENT UNDER A FEW YEARS LATER. THE BUILDING WAS USED AS A LIVERY STABLE UNTIL IT BURNED DOWN IN 1865.

51

Prior to the 1870's there were no night nurses at Bellevue Hospital. Instead, three night watchmen made rounds among some 800 patients. In 1874 Miss Linda Richards became night superintendent and she introduced the practice of keeping records on patients and issuing written instructions for nurses on her staff.

To Be a Nurse

Born in New York City in 1837, Louisa Lee Schuyler was the great-granddaughter of General Philip Schuyler and Alexander Hamilton.

IN 1798 DR. VALENTINE SEAMAN WAS THE **FIRST** PERSON IN THE U.S. TO START A SCHOOL TO TRAIN NURSES. HE TAUGHT ANATOMY, PHYSIOLOGY, CARE OF CHILDREN, AND MIDWIFERY TO ABOUT TWO DOZEN STUDENTS IN THE NEW YORK HOSPITAL ON WEST 15th STREET NEAR 5th AVENUE.

THERE WERE VIRTUALLY NO NURSING SCHOOLS IN THE COUNTRY FOR THE NEXT 70 YEARS, AND THE PROFESSION SUFFERED.

NURSING WAS CONSIDERED SO DEGRADING THAT THE ONLY PEOPLE WILLING TO DO IT WERE FEMALE EX-CONVICTS.

HERE'S YER SUPPER!

THEY DEMANDED FEES FROM THEIR PATIENTS FOR THEIR CRUDE SERVICES. DRUNKENNESS AND FOUL LANGUAGE WERE COMMON.

THAT'LL BE TWO CENTS, YA OL' BAT!

LOUISA LEE SCHUYLER & OTHER PROMINENT WOMEN FORMED THE NEW YORK STATE CHARITIES AID ASSN. IN 1872 TO CARE FOR PAUPERS, ORPHANS, & THE SICK.

NEXT, MISS SCHUYLER ASKED THE COMMISSIONERS OF CHARITY TO SET UP A SCHOOL TO TRAIN NURSES.

AFTER STALLING FOR A YEAR THE COMMISSIONERS RELUCTANTLY ALLOWED LOUISA THE USE OF 6 WARDS IN BELLEVUE HOSPITAL AS A SCHOOL FOR NURSES.

The first director of the Bellevue Nursing School was Sister Helen Bowden of the Sisterhood of All Saints. She was trained at the University College Hospital in London, one of Florence Nightingale's schools. Thus, she introduced the Nightingale System to America which became known as the "Bellevue System." Sister Helen left Bellevue in May, 1876.

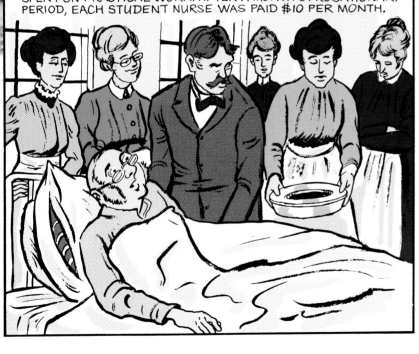

LOUISA LEE SCHUYLER FOUNDED THE BELLEVUE HOSPITAL

TRAINING SCHOOL FOR NURSES

IN MAY, 1873. FIVE STUDENTS ENROLLED IN THE FIRST CLASS, BUT THERE WERE FEW LECTURES. MOST OF THEIR TIME WAS SPENT ON PRACTICAL WORK. AFTER A MONTH'S PROBATIONARY PERIOD, EACH STUDENT NURSE WAS PAID $10 PER MONTH.

NO NURSE HAD EVER WORN A UNIFORM UNTIL A WEALTHY STUDENT HAD ONE MADE FOR HERSELF IN 1874. HER NAME WAS EUPHEMIA VAN RENSSELAER, A DESCENDANT OF A DUTCH PATROON.

WITHIN A WEEK, EVERY NURSE WAS WEARING A UNIFORM AND IT HAS BEEN A STANDARD PRACTICE EVER SINCE.

BELLEVUE BECAME ONE OF THE FINEST NURSING SCHOOLS IN THE WORLD. SOME OF ITS DISTINGUISHED GRADUATES INCLUDE:

LAVINIA DOCK, AUTHOR OF THE FIRST TEXTBOOK ON NURSING.

MARY SNIVELY, A FOUNDER OF THE CANADIAN NURSING ASSN.

JANE DELANO, HER STORY NEXT WEEK.

During the yellow fever epidemic of 1887-88, Jane Delano served as superintendent nurse at an emergency center near Jacksonville, Florida. Even though the source of the disease had not yet been discovered, she insisted on the use of mosquito netting in the center.

Red Cross Nurse

Miss Delano also did a stint as superintendent of the Army Nurse Corps in the early 1900's. Her salary was $40 per month for duty in the US and $50 per month for duty elsewhere.

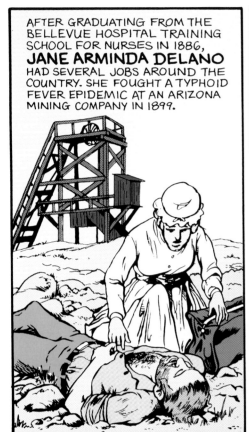

AFTER GRADUATING FROM THE BELLEVUE HOSPITAL TRAINING SCHOOL FOR NURSES IN 1886, **JANE ARMINDA DELANO** HAD SEVERAL JOBS AROUND THE COUNTRY. SHE FOUGHT A TYPHOID FEVER EPIDEMIC AT AN ARIZONA MINING COMPANY IN 1899.

SHE RETURNED TO NEW YORK IN 1900 TO DIRECT THE GIRLS DEPARTMENT OF THE NEW YORK CITY HOUSE OF REFUGE ON **RANDALL'S ISLAND.**

FROM 1902 TO 1906 JANE RAN THE BELLEVUE HOSPITAL NURSING SCHOOL.

THE AMERICAN RED CROSS NURSING SERVICE WAS ORGANIZED IN 1909 AND JANE DELANO WAS ITS CHAIRMAN FOR THE NEXT TEN YEARS.

WHEN AMERICA ENTERED WORLD WAR I IN APRIL, 1917, MISS DELANO SUPERVISED THE MOBILIZATION OF OVER 20,000 NURSES PLUS HUNDREDS OF NURSE'S AIDES AND OTHER WORKERS FOR DUTY OVERSEAS.

THE SHOOTING WAR STOPPED IN 1918, BUT JANE DELANO AND HER NURSES FACED ANOTHER BATTLE-THE GREAT INFLUENZA EPIDEMIC THAT PLAGUED EUROPE AND AMERICA.

FATIGUE AND EXHAUSTION OVERTOOK JANE ON AN INSPECTION TOUR.

SHE DIED IN SAVENAY, FRANCE ON APRIL 15, 1919, LEAVING AN ESTATE OF $50,000. MOST OF IT WENT TO THE *DELANO RED CROSS NURSING SERVICE.*

The "catch" to Dr. Kennion's free coffee and bread was that its recipients had to listen to one of his sermons.

Many regarded this as free entertainment because Kennion was such a dynamic speaker.

The Coffee Crusade

DR. JOHN W. KENNION, FORMERLY A JOURNALIST IN BROOKLYN, SHOWN IN FRONT OF THE BANNER, HELPED THE POOR AND NEGLECTED OF NEW YORK IN THE 1870's AND 80's.

HIS SUCCESS WAS DUE TO THE COMMON SENSE METHOD OF HIS WORK. HE FOUND SHELTER FOR THE HOMELESS, FED THE HUNGRY, CLOTHED THE NEEDY, AND GOT JOBS FOR OTHERS.

TO FIGHT ALCOHOLISM HE ROAMED THE CITY WITH HIS SPECIALLY DESIGNED **COFFEE URN CART** AND OFFERED FREE COFFEE AND FRESH BREAD AS AN ALTERNATIVE FOR BOOZE.

KENNION CLAIMED, "A CUP OF COFFEE GIVEN ON A COLD DAY TO SOME POOR WRETCH MIGHT PREVENT A SUICIDE OR A MURDER, AND COULD GO TOWARD REDEEMING A FALLEN MAN."

THIS SCENE IS THE SQUARE OPPOSITE THE ROOSEVELT STREET FERRY IN MANHATTAN ON A SUNDAY IN 1880.

FREE AND BREAD FREE

The first submarine was a leather-covered rowboat constructed in England around 1620 by Cornelius Van Drebbel, a Dutch scientist.
Robert Fulton built the *Nautilus,* a 21 foot, copper-clad sub in 1800. He tried to sell it to the French but Napoleon was not interested.

The Story of the Submarine

JOHN PHILIP **HOLLAND,** A SCHOOLTEACHER IN COUNTY CLARE DURING THE 1860's, BELIEVED HE COULD HELP IRELAND GAIN INDEPENDENCE FROM ENGLAND BY INVENTING A SUBMARINE THAT WOULD DESTROY THE BRITISH FLEET.

HIS NEIGHBORS THOUGHT HE WAS CRAZY, AND NOBODY WOULD INVEST IN HIS IDEA.

AT AGE 32, IN 1873, HE CAME TO AMERICA AND GOT A JOB AS A TEACHER IN PATERSON, NEW JERSEY.

TWO YEARS LATER HE BUILT HIS FIRST SUB IN THE PATERSON WORKSHOP OF TWO OF HIS FRIENDS, MESSRS. TODD AND RAFFERTY.

HOLLAND TOOK IT ON SOME EXPERIMENTAL DIVES IN THE PASSAIC RIVER. HE SAT IN THE MIDDLE, HIS FEET WORKING PEDALS THAT TURNED THE PROPELLOR.

HE LAUNCHED A SECOND SUB IN 1878, BUT IT BECAME IMMEDIATELY STUCK IN THE MUD.

IT ALSO LEAKED CONSTANTLY AND ITS FOUR-HORSEPOWER ENGINE WAS UNRELIABLE.

REALIZING HE HAD TO BUILD A BETTER MODEL, HOLLAND SANK THIS SUB UNDER THE *FALLS BRIDGE* IN PATERSON. IN 1927 SOME COLLEGE MEN RAISED THE SUB AND SOLD IT FOR SCRAP.

Meanwhile, a man named Drzewiecki was working on a submarine for the Russians. In 1876 he put together the *Podascophe II*, a pedal-powered sub measuring 16 feet. The Czar's government was said to have ordered eight of them.

The Sinn Fein's Submarine

IN 1880 THE SINN FEIN PAID JOHN HOLLAND, AN IRISH SCHOOLTEACHER IN PATERSON, NJ, TO INVENT A SUBMARINE THAT WOULD SINK THE BRITISH FLEET. THE SINN FEIN, OR FENIANS, WAS A SECRET SOCIETY BENT ON ESTABLISHING A REPUBLIC OF IRELAND BY FORCE.

HOLLAND BUILT A THREE-MAN SUBMARINE AT THE DELAMATER IRON WORKS AT THE FOOT OF WEST 13th STREET IN MANHATTAN.

THE *FENIAN RAM* WAS LAUNCHED IN MAY, 1881 AND DIVED ALMOST DAILY IN NEW YORK HARBOR.

MR. HOLLAND WAS THE FIRST PERSON TO BUILD A BUOYANT SUBMARINE WHICH COULD COMPLETELY NAVIGATE UNDER WATER: UP, DOWN, PORT, STARBOARD AND FORWARD.

MEANWHILE, THE FENIANS IN IRELAND DECIDED TO PEACEFULLY NEGOTIATE WITH ENGLAND FOR HOME RULE. CONSEQUENTLY...

WE'RE NOT SPENDIN' ANYMORE MONEY ON WARSHIPS THAT WE'LL NEVER USE!

SOME OF THE FENIANS IN AMERICA HATED TO SEE THEIR SUBMARINE PROJECT GO DOWN THE DRAIN, SO THEY SEIZED THE *RAM* AND TOOK IT TO NEW HAVEN, CT., AND STASHED IT IN A SHED OWNED BY ONE OF THEIR MEMBERS.

TODAY THE *FENIAN RAM* IS ON DISPLAY IN PATERSON, N.J.

The Sinn Fein paid Holland $4,000 to design their submarine. After someone recovered the *Fenian Ram* from that shed in Connecticut, it was used as an instructional aid at the Merchant Marine Academy on Long Island. It is now part of the memorial to John Holland in Westside Park, Paterson, NJ pictured in the last panel on page 59.

The Elusive Contract

AFTER THE IRISH SECRET SOCIETY KNOWN AS THE SINN FEIN ABSCONDED WITH THEIR SUBMARINE, INVENTOR JOHN P. HOLLAND BUILT ANOTHER SUB AND TESTED IT IN NEW YORK HARBOR DURING THE 1880's.

IN 1888, SECRETARY OF THE NAVY WM. C. WHITNEY CONVINCED HIS BOSS, PRESIDENT GROVER CLEVELAND, THAT THE NAVY NEEDED SUBMARINES.

SEVERAL INVENTORS SUBMITTED DESIGNS AND HOLLAND'S WAS SELECTED, BUT...

BEFORE THE CONTRACT WAS SIGNED, BENJAMIN HARRISON WAS SWORN IN AS PRESIDENT, AND HE CANCELLED THE PROJECT.

DURING THE NEXT FIVE YEARS, HOLLAND BUILT FIVE MORE SUBMARINES, USING ALL HIS OWN MONEY AND WHATEVER HE COULD BORROW.

CLEVELAND BECAME PRESIDENT AGAIN IN 1893 AND THE SUBMARINE PROGRAM WAS ON AGAIN. INVENTORS WERE INVITED TO SUBMIT DESIGNS.

AT LUNCH WITH A YOUNG LAWYER IN A DOWNTOWN NEW YORK RESTAURANT, HOLLAND REMARKED,

I CAN WIN THAT CONTRACT TO BUILD THE NAVY'S SUB IF I COULD RAISE $347.19 FOR FEES AND EXPENSES.

WHAT'S THE NINETEEN CENTS FOR?

TO BUY A CERTAIN KIND OF RULER I NEED FOR DRAWING MY PLANS.

IF YOU FIGURED IT THAT CLOSELY, *I'LL* LOAN YOU THE MONEY!

HE DID SO, IN EXCHANGE FOR A LARGE BLOCK OF STOCK IN THE NEW *HOLLAND TORPEDO BOAT CO.* AT 100 BROADWAY. TODAY, THAT STOCK IS WORTH MILLIONS.

Mr. Holland almost started the Spanish-American War himself. During the spring of 1898, tensions were running high between the US and Spain, so the US sent the battleship *Maine* to Havana, Cuba, a Spanish colony at the time. In protest, the Spanish anchored its warship *Viscaya* in New York Harbor. Holland was testing one of his subs in the harbor at the time and he toyed with the idea of attacking the *Viscaya*. However, somebody convinced him it would not be a good idea.

The Navy's First Submarine

JOHN P. HOLLAND OF PATERSON, NJ WON A $200,000 CONTRACT TO BUILD THE NAVY'S FIRST SUBMARINE IN 1893. AFTER A TWO YEAR DELAY, HIS COMPANY, THE HOLLAND TORPEDO BOAT COMPANY AT 100 BROADWAY, BEGAN CONSTRUCTION ON THE *PLUNGER* IN BALTIMORE, MD.

THE *PLUNGER* WAS LAUNCHED IN 1897, BUT HOLLAND FORESAW ITS DEFECTS, SO HE DID SOMETHING UNHEARD OF TODAY:

HE RETURNED ALL THE MONEY THE GOVERNMENT HAD SPENT ON THE *PLUNGER* AND DESIGNED A NEW BOAT.

HIS NEW BOAT WAS A SUCCESS. BUILT AT THE CRESCENT SHIPYARD IN ELIZABETHPORT, N.J., THE *HOLLAND* WAS LAUNCHED IN EARLY SPRING, 1898.

AFTER TEST RUNS OFF STATEN ISLAND, THE NAVY'S FIRST SUB WAS COMMISSIONED ON OCTOBER 13, 1900.

CUTAWAY VIEW

FOR MANY YEARS THEREAFTER, HOLLAND'S FIRM BUILT MOST OF THE U.S. NAVY'S SUBMARINES, AND MANY FOR THE NAVIES OF FOREIGN POWERS.

JOHN HOLLAND DIED IN AUGUST, 1914, A YEAR BEFORE THE U.S. NAVY SCRAPPED ITS FIRST SUBMARINE.

THIS MONUMENT TO MR. HOLLAND NOW STANDS IN WESTSIDE PARK, PATERSON, N.J.

59

Mr. Richardson's daughter inherited the infamous house in this story. Later, others purchased it and incorporated it into the adjoining building.

JOSEPH RICHARDSON, A WEALTHY CONTRACTOR, OWNED A SMALL LOT AT THE CORNER OF LEXINGTON AVENUE & EAST 82nd STREET, MEASURING 5 FEET WIDE BY 100 FEET DEEP. THE NEXT DOOR NEIGHBOR OFFERED TO BUY IT.

I'LL GIVE YOU $1,000 FOR THE LOT.

I WON'T TAKE A CENT LESS THAN $5,000!

THE NEIGHBOR REFUSED TO PAY $5,000. THIS REALLY **INFURIATED** RICHARDSON.

I'LL SHOW THAT BUM. I'LL BUILD MY OWN HOUSE ON THAT LOT!

CONSTRUCTION OF THE HOUSE WAS COMPLETED IN 1892 AND RICHARDSON MOVED IN.

The SPITE House

INSIDE, THE STAIRS WERE SO NARROW THAT TWO PEOPLE COULD NOT PASS ONE ANOTHER.

THE DINING ROOM TABLE WAS ONLY 18 INCHES WIDE, AND THE BEDS WERE NOT MUCH WIDER.

MR. RICHARDSON DIED IN HIS "SPITE HOUSE" IN 1897 AT AGE 84. HE WAS REPUTED TO HAVE BEEN WORTH OVER $20 MILLION.

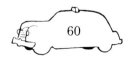

D. H. Burnham & Co., a well-known architectural firm in Chicago, pioneered the design of skyscrapers utilizing steel skeletons. One of the first buildings to use this new concept of steel girder construction is depicted here.

The Winds of 23rd St.

Originally named the Fuller Building after its developer, the 20-story Flatiron Building was the tallest skyscraper in New York for many years.

THE **FLATIRON** BUILDING WAS ERECTED IN 1902 WHERE BROADWAY CROSSES FIFTH AVENUE AND 23rd STREET.

ITS UNIQUE CONFIGURATION MADE IT THE MOST FAMOUS SKYSCRAPER IN THE WORLD FOR MANY YEARS.

THE FLATIRON WAS ALSO POPULAR FOR CAUSING ATMOSPHERIC ACROBATICS. MILD BREEZES THAT SWIRLED PAST THIS TRIANGULAR STRUCTURE PICKED UP SPEED AND DID A NUMBER ON PASSERS-BY, MUCH TO THE GLEE OF SPECTATORS WHO HUDDLED IN ITS DOORWAYS.

THE COPS AROUND 23rd STREET CHASED AWAY THESE GAWKERS BY USING AN EXPRESSION THAT HAS BECOME A PART OF AMERICAN SLANG FOR *GET MOVING*...

TWENTY-THREE SKIDOO!

61

As a 12 year-old in Wisconsin in 1893, Ted Snyder supported his mother and sister by playing the piano. He came to New York in 1904 and got a job with the F. A. Mills Company. Four years later he started his own firm, the Ted Snyder Company, financially backed by Henry Waterson of the Crown Music Company. In 1908 he published his first big hit, a rag called *Wild Cherries*.

The Singing Waiter

In 1921, Ted Snyder wrote a song based on a best-selling book at the time, *The Sheik*. It became Snyder's biggest hit - *The Sheik of Araby*.

TED SNYDER, A PIANIST AND SONG PLUGGER FROM CHICAGO CAME TO NEW YORK AND, IN 1908, STARTED HIS OWN MUSIC PUBLISHING COMPANY AT 112 WEST 38th ST. ONE DAY AMY BUTLER, A SINGER, PAID HIM A VISIT.

YOU'VE GOT TO MEET THIS SINGING WAITER. HE WRITES TERRIFIC LYRICS AND COULD BE USEFUL TO YOUR BUSINESS!

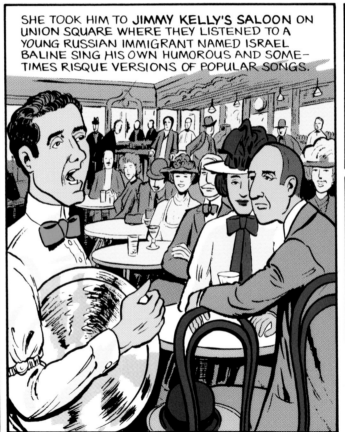

SHE TOOK HIM TO JIMMY KELLY'S SALOON ON UNION SQUARE WHERE THEY LISTENED TO A YOUNG RUSSIAN IMMIGRANT NAMED ISRAEL BALINE SING HIS OWN HUMOROUS AND SOMETIMES RISQUE VERSIONS OF POPULAR SONGS.

SNYDER WAS NOT VERY IMPRESSED, BUT MISS BUTLER KEPT AFTER HIM UNTIL FINALLY...

SNYDER HIRED BALINE TO WRITE SONGS FOR A WEEKLY DRAW OF $25 AGAINST FUTURE ROYALTIES. IT WAS A GREAT DECISION BECAUSE A YEAR EARLIER IZZY BALINE HAD CHANGED HIS NAME TO IRVING BERLIN.

Elda Furry was born on June 2, 1890 in Hollidaysburg, PA. She was bitten by the show-biz bug around 1906 when she saw Ethel Barrymore on tour in nearby Altoona, PA doing *Captain Jinks and the Horse Marines.*

Meanwhile, her husband-to-be, DeWolf Hopper, was already a star, famous for his recitals of *Casey at the Bat.*

The Plain Girl From Hollidaysburg, Pa.

STAGE-STRUCK AS A TEENAGER, **ELDA** LEFT HER STRICT *PLAIN BRETHREN* HOME AT 17 AND WENT TO STAY WITH HER UNCLE SAM IN NEW YORK.

HER FIRST JOB WAS IN THE CHORUS OF THE ABORN OPERA COMPANY.

SHE MADE HER DEBUT ON BROADWAY IN THE CHORUS OF *THE MOTOR GIRL* IN 1909.

ALONG THE WAY SHE MET DEWOLF HOPPER, ONE OF THE BIGGEST STARS ON BROADWAY.

HOPPER WAS FOUR YEARS OLDER THAN ELDA'S FATHER. NEVERTHE-LESS...

ELDA BECAME HOPPER'S **5th WIFE** IN 1913. THEY LIVED IN THE ALGONQUIN HOTEL ON W. 44th ST.

HOPPER'S FORMER WIVES WERE:

IDA

ELLA

NELLA   EDNA

THIS LED TO CONFUSION.

WHAT TIME IS IT, NELLA... ER, EDNA...I MEAN ELDA...

ELDA WENT TO A NUMEROLOGIST WHO COMBINED DATES AND NUMBERS AND CAME UP WITH A NEW NAME, **HEDDA HOPPER!**

HEDDA HOPPER BECAME A SYNDICATED COLUMNIST COVERING HOLLYWOOD. AS SUCH, SHE WAS ONE OF THE MOST INFLUENTIAL, AND FEARED, PERSONALITIES IN THE ENTERTAINMENT BUSINESS.

Here are some items that made the headlines in 1947:
A ship exploded in Texas City, TX killing over 500 people and virtually annihilating the city.
Jackie Robinson became the first African-American in 20th century major league baseball when he signed with the Brooklyn Dodgers of the National League.

The Big News of 1947

Two hit musicals opened on Broadway in 1947: *Finian's Rainbow* by E. Y. Harburg, a fantasy about an old Irishman who had stolen a crock of gold from a leprechaun; *Brigadoon* by Alan J. Lerner, concerning two Americans in a small Scottish town.

THE UNITED NATIONS REVEALED ITS PLANS TO BUILD ITS HEADQUARTERS IN MIDTOWN MANHATTAN. BUT THAT WAS NOT THE BIG NEWS.

HENRY FORD DIED AT THE AGE OF 83 IN HIS MANSION IN DEARBORN, MICHIGAN. BUT THAT WAS NOT THE BIG NEWS.

OVER 300,000 TELEPHONE WORKERS WENT ON THE FIRST NATIONWIDE STRIKE, CRIPPLING LONG DISTANCE CALLS.

OPERATOR...HELLO... HELLO...

NOR WAS THAT THE BIG NEWS.

THE BIG NEWS OF 1947 WAS ABOUT AMERICA'S FOREMOST PACK RATS, THE **COLLYER BROTHERS!**

ON MARCH 21st, POLICE DISCOVERED THE DEAD BODY OF HOMER IN THEIR JUNK-FILLED HOUSE IN HARLEM. MYSTERIOUSLY MISSING WAS HIS BROTHER, LANGLEY, FOR WHOM A MULTI-STATE MANHUNT WAS LAUNCHED.

THE COLLYER FAMILY

Dr. Herman Collyer claimed his ancestors came to America in 1620 on the *Mayflower*.

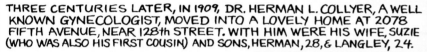

THREE CENTURIES LATER, IN 1909, DR. HERMAN L. COLLYER, A WELL KNOWN GYNECOLOGIST, MOVED INTO A LOVELY HOME AT 2078 FIFTH AVENUE, NEAR 128th STREET. WITH HIM WERE HIS WIFE, SUZIE (WHO WAS ALSO HIS FIRST COUSIN) AND SONS, HERMAN, 28, & LANGLEY, 24.

THE DOCTOR WAS CONSIDERED A BIT ECCENTRIC. IT WAS SAID...

HE USED TO PADDLE TO WORK AT CITY HOSPITAL ON BLACKWELL'S ISLAND.

THEN, HE CARRIED HIS CANOE HOME AT NIGHT.

THE COLLYER BROTHERS NEVER MARRIED. HOMER ATTENDED CITY COLLEGE OF NEW YORK AND WAS AN ADMIRALTY LAWYER FOR YEARS.

LANGLEY STUDIED ENGINEERING AT COLUMBIA UNIVERSITY, BUT NEVER WORKED FOR A LIVING. SUZIE CONSTANTLY FUSSED OVER HER SONS. CONTINUED...

For a time, Langley wanted to be a concert pianist. "I played in public often," Langley said. "My last concert was in Carnegie Hall, a week before Paderewski's first. He got more notices than I, so I gave up. What's the use?" He never played before an audience again.

A FAMILY IN DISARRAY

THE COLLYERS SEEMED TO BE A CLOSE-KNIT FAMILY. BY 1920, BROTHERS HOMER AND LANGLEY WERE BACHELORS IN THEIR THIRTIES, STILL LIVING WITH THEIR PARENTS AT 2078 FIFTH AVENUE. THEN, SUDDENLY, THEIR FATHER LEFT AND MOVED INTO A HOUSE AT 153 WEST 77th STREET.

NOT LONG AFTERWARD SUZIE, THEIR MOTHER, LEFT. IT IS NOT KNOWN IF SHE JOINED HER HUSBAND OR STAYED WITH RELATIVES.

A SHORT TIME LATER, IN 1923, THEIR FATHER DIED, LEAVING HIS SONS AN ESTATE WORTH ABOUT $100,000 INCLUDING A SUMMER COTTAGE IN QUEENS WHICH THEY NEVER VISITED.

SOMEWHERE BETWEEN THE DEATH OF THEIR FATHER AND THAT OF THEIR MOTHER IN 1929, HOMER AND LANGLEY STARTED TO ACT STRANGELY. THEY REFUSED TO PAY THEIR BILLS OR ALLOW ANYONE TO SET FOOT INTO THEIR HOUSE. THEIR GAS, WATER, HEAT, AND ELECTRICITY WERE SHUT OFF.

The Hermits of Harlem

IN 1932 HOMER COLLYER BOUGHT A HOUSE AT 2077 FIFTH AVE., ACROSS THE STREET FROM HIS OWN. HE PAID $8,000 IN CASH AND PLANNED TO CONVERT IT INTO APARTMENTS.

BUT HE NEVER DID ANYTHING ABOUT THE HOUSE BECAUSE, IN 1933, HE SUFFERED HEMORRHAGES IN BOTH EYES AND WENT BLIND.

LANGLEY DEVOTED HIMSELF TO CARING FOR HIS BROTHER. HE NEVER CALLED A DOCTOR, BELIEVING HE COULD CURE HOMER BY FEEDING HIM DOZENS OF ORANGES A WEEK.

IT DID NOT WORK.

SOMETIMES LANGLEY VENTURED INTO THE NIGHT SCROUNGING FOR ALL KINDS OF JUNK.

LANGLEY ALSO HOARDED TONS OF NEWSPAPERS BECAUSE...

HOMER CAN CATCH UP ON THE NEWS WHEN HE REGAINS HIS SIGHT.

When Homer Collyer's health began to fail, his brother, Langley, devoted his life to caring for him. Langley never sought help from a physician, claiming he could just consult any of the 15,000 medical books their father had left in the house.

67

One of the Collyer's few acquaintances said, "In 1933 I walked around the block with Homer. He told me he was going blind and would never come out of the house again. He seemed resigned, and said there was no use going out if he couldn't see, no use working if he couldn't read."

The Model T in the Cellar

SOME TIME DURING THE 1930's THE HOUSE ON WEST 77th ST. WHERE DR. HERMAN COLLYER (AND POSSIBLY HIS WIFE) DIED, WAS SOLD. THE NEW OWNER, A MRS. PETER MEYER, FOUND IN THE CELLAR AN OLD MODEL T FORD THAT COULD NOT BE REMOVED INTACT. SHE PAID A MAN $100 TO DISMANTLE IT AND PUT THE PARTS ON THE SIDEWALK WITH THE TRASH.

DR. COLLYER'S SON, LANGLEY, HEARD ABOUT IT AND, PIECE BY PIECE, SCHLEPPED THE CAR UP-TOWN AND PUT IT IN HIS OWN BASEMENT.

THE ELECTRICITY IN LANGLEY'S HOUSE HAD BEEN SHUT OFF, SO HE TRIED TO HOOK UP A GENERATOR TO THE CAR'S ENGINE, BUT IT DID NOT WORK.

MEANWHILE, THE COLLYER HOME ON FIFTH AVENUE WAS FILLING UP WITH THE "REWARDS" OF LANGLEY'S NIGHTLY FORAYS FOR JUNK: DISCARDED FURNITURE, ICE-BOXES, BABY CARRIAGES, ANIMAL BONES, AND BOXES OF FOUL-SMELLING CLOTHES.

AN ACCOMPLISHED PIANIST, LANGLEY ENTERTAINED HIS BLIND BROTHER BY PLAYING A PIPE ORGAN OR ONE OF ELEVEN PIANOS INCLUDING ONE GIVEN TO THEIR MOTHER BY QUEEN VICTORIA.

There was no indication of how Langley entered or left his cluttered house on his daily shopping trips to buy food for his ailing brother. The neighbors insisted he came and went through the front basement door, but the police who later searched the house said it could not be done.

MAZES AND BOOBY TRAPS

FOR OVER A DOZEN YEARS HOMER AND LANGLEY COLLYER HAD SECLUDED THEMSELVES IN THEIR JUNK-FILLED HOUSE ON FIFTH AVENUE.

THEN, IN 1942, A RUMOR CIRCULATED THAT HOMER WAS LYING DEAD INSIDE THE HOUSE.

HOMER'S OLD FRIEND, SGT. JOHN COLLINS, DECIDED TO INVESTIGATE.

COLLINS PURSUADED LANGLEY TO LET HIM IN.

FOLLOW ME, BUT BE CAREFUL!

TO PROTECT US FROM BURGLARS, I RIGGED SOME BOOBY TRAPS.

ALL A THIEF HAS TO DO IS BUMP ONE OF THESE TRIP WIRES AND HUNDREDS OF POUNDS OF STUFF WILL FALL AND CRUSH HIM!

A HALF-HOUR LATER THEY REACHED THE ROOM WHERE HOMER WAS.

I AM HOMER COLLYER. I WANT YOUR NAME AND SHIELD NUMBER. I AM NOT DEAD!

LATER, LANGLEY COMPLAINED TO THE POLICE DE-PARTMENT FOR THE "INTRUSION."

69

Homer Collyer was seen outside for the last time on January 1, 1940. Sgt. Collins of the city police, who had been keeping an eye on the brothers for several years, saw Homer and Langley carrying the limb of an old elm tree across the street to the basement of their house. Homer held on to one end of the branch as Langley led the way.

Kings of the Pack Rats

Over the years, the police received calls saying that someone was dead in the Collyer mansion. They always investigated because sooner or later one of the calls would be accurate.

THE COLLYER BROTHERS' ISOLATION WAS RUDELY INTERRUPTED WHEN THE BOWERY SAVINGS BANK FORECLOSED ON A MORTGAGE FOR $6,700 PLUS INTEREST IN JULY, 1942.

WITH TONS OF JUNK BLOCKING THE ENTRANCES A DEPUTY SHERIFF HAD TO CLIMB TO THE SECOND STORY TO DELIVER THE EVICTION NOTICE.

WAITING INSIDE WERE HOMER AND LANGLEY ALONG WITH THEIR LAWYER, JOHN McMULLEN.

DON'T COME ANY FURTHER. HERE'S YOUR MONEY.✱ PLEASE LEAVE.

✱SAID TO HAVE BEEN A CHECK FOR $10,000.

NEXT, THE FEDERAL GOVERNMENT CAME AFTER THE COLLYERS FOR NON-PAYMENT OF TAXES.

THE FEDS SEIZED THE HOUSE AT 2077 FIFTH AVENUE (THE ONE HOMER BOUGHT AS AN INVESTMENT) AND PUT IT UP FOR PUBLIC AUCTION.

THERE WERE NO TAKERS, SO THE GOVERNMENT WAS STUCK WITH IT.

THROUGH ALL THIS THE COLLYERS REMAINED SHY AND GENTLE MEN. SOMETIMES LANGLEY SAT ON HIS STOOP & CHATTED WITH NEIGHBORS.

THEN, ON MAR. 21, 1947, THE POLICE RECEIVED A CALL...

THERE'S A MAN DEAD IN THE COLLYER HOUSE.

The man who made the call identified himself as William Smith. It turned out that he really was William Rodriquo of 1 West Street, a friend of the Collyers.

WILLIAM BARKER JOINED NEW YORK'S FINEST IN 1941, BUT LEFT A YEAR LATER TO FIGHT IN WORLD WAR II. HE RETURNED IN 1946 AND WAS ON HIS BEAT IN HARLEM WHEN THE CALL CAME TO INVESTIGATE A REPORT OF A DEAD BODY AT 2078 FIFTH AVENUE.

BARKER SUMMONED EMERGENCY SQUAD No. SIX AT 10 A.M. THEY BROKE DOWN EVERY EXTERIOR DOOR BUT COULD NOT GET INSIDE BECAUSE THEY WERE BLOCKED BY TONS OF JUNK.

DEAD ON ARRIVAL*

AROUND NOON THEY CALLED THE FIRE DEPARTMENT AND PATROLMAN WILLIAM BARKER CLIMBED ONE OF THEIR LADDERS TO THE SECOND STORY.

INSIDE THE AWFUL STENCH HIT HIM LIKE A TRUCK.

BARKER QUICKLY RETURNED TO THE WINDOW.

Over the years, Mr. Barker refused to be interviewed by the news media about the recluses. But, alone with his family, Barker always spoke kindly of the two old gents whom he regarded as his friends.

HE KNOCKED ON THE DOOR BUT NOBODY ANSWERED.

THERE'S A D.O.A.* HERE!

DETECTIVES JOE WHITMORE AND JOHN LOUGHERY OF THE 123rd ST. STATION CLIMBED INTO THE ROOM AND IDENTIFIED THE BODY.

IT'S HOMER COLLYER.

The basement of the Collyer house was so crammed with junk that it was hard to see how anything other than the numerous rats could squeeze through. The entrance contained an old stove, several umbrellas, countless bundles of newspapers, a gas mask canister, an old stove pipe, and a broken scooter.

Through the Roof

HOMER COLLYER WAS FOUND DEAD OF STARVATION IN HIS HOUSE ON FIFTH AVENUE AROUND NOON, MAR. 21, 1947. IMMEDIATELY THE POLICE BEGAN TO SEARCH FOR LANGLEY, HIS BROTHER, BY THROWING OUT TONS OF JUNK. TWO TONS OF STUFF HAD BEEN CARTED OFF TO THE DUMP BEFORE JOHN LOUGHERY, THE DETECTIVE IN CHARGE, INTERVENED...

DON'T TOUCH ANYMORE JUNK. THE RELATIVES MIGHT SAY IT'S WORTH $1,000.

AT 1:14 PM, THE BROTHERS' LAWYER, JOHN R. McMULLEN, AND THE FIRST OF SOME 40 COLLYER RELATIVES ARRIVED ON THE SCENE.

YOU MAY SEARCH THE HOUSE FOR LANGLEY BUT BE CAREFUL. HE'S TERRIFIED OF INTRUDERS AND MIGHT BE IN THERE WITH A GUN.

THE POLICE STARTED THEIR SEARCH BY DROPPING THROUGH THE SKYLIGHT BECAUSE THE LOWER FLOORS AND STAIRS WERE JAMMED WITH DEBRIS AND BOOBY TRAPS.

FOR TWO WEEKS THEY SIFTED THROUGH 120 TONS OF JUNK, CAREFUL NOT TO DESTROY ANYTHING. THEY WORKED IN FIFTEEN MINUTE SHIFTS BECAUSE THE STENCH OF ROT, MILDEW, AND HUMAN WASTE WAS UNBEARABLE.

Some of the "treasures" that Langley had saved included: oyster shells from 1890 banquets, the jawbone of a horse, kneepads for bowlegged acrobats, protests against women's suffrage, high hats, Victorian bustles, and early colonial furniture. By 1947 Langley had accumulated eleven grand pianos and a huge ancient pump organ.

The Collyers' assets totaled at least $100,000 on deposit in many banks. During the search of the mansion, police found 34 bank books with deposits totalling $3,007.18.

THE HUNT FOR LANGLEY

FOR THREE WEEKS IN THE SPRING OF 1947 NEW YORK'S FINEST SEARCHED THE COLLYER MANSION ON FIFTH AVENUE FOR THE MISSING BROTHER, LANGLEY. DAY AFTER DAY ONLOOKERS, MANY FROM NEW JERSEY AND CONNECTICUT, WATCHED AND WAITED FOR SOMETHING EXCITING TO HAPPEN. SIGHTSEEING BUSES ADDED THE COLLYER HOUSE TO THEIR RUBBERNECKING ROUTES.

THE ENTIRE AFFAIR CREATED A NEWS MEDIA FRENZY. REPORTERS FROM ALL OVER THE COUNTRY COVERED THE STORY ALONG WITH THE RADIO NETWORKS AND MOVIE NEWSREELS.

THE MANHUNT FOR LANGLEY SPREAD TO ELEVEN STATES. THEN, ON APRIL 8, DETECTIVES, SEARCHING JUST TEN FEET FROM WHERE HOMER'S BODY HAD BEEN FOUND, MADE A GRUESOME DISCOVERY.

HAVE YOU SEEN THIS MAN?

LANGLEY COLLYER

IT'S LANGLEY—CAUGHT IN ONE OF HIS TRAPS.

Laborers from the Public Administrator's office and detectives removed the debris from the Collyer house. Items of no value, at times 17 tons per day, were carted away by the Department of Sanitation. The rest were stored in a building downtown until they were sold at auction.

The cops also found a small arsenal of weapons, all oiled and in good condition: rifles, pistols, a sabre, and a French bayonet.

WHAT HAPPENED TO LANGLEY

IN LATE FEBRUARY, 1947, LANGLEY COLLYER WAS CRAWLING THROUGH A TUNNEL OF JUNK BRINGING FOOD TO HIS BROTHER, HOMER, WHEN ACCIDENTLY...

SNAP!

HE TRIPPED ONE OF HIS OWN **BOOBY TRAPS!**

UNABLE TO MOVE, LANGLEY WAS SMOTHERED TO DEATH BY THE JUNK THAT FELL ON HIM.

HOMER, BLIND AND PARALYZED, HUNG ON FOR A FEW WEEKS, THEN DIED OF STARVATION AND DEHYDRATION. WHEN FOUND, HOMER'S GNARLED FINGERS WERE STRETCHED TOWARD HIS DEAD BROTHER'S "TOMB."

ON APRIL 12, 1947 LANGLEY COLLYER WAS BURIED NEXT TO HIS BROTHER AND THEIR PARENTS IN CYPRESS HILLS CEMETERY IN QUEENS.

The manhunt for Langley spawned rumors from Massachusetts to Georgia. People reported seeing the recluse in restaurants, on the beach in Atlantic City, and even hitch-hiking.

Langley had been dead for over a month when he was found. Rats had gnawed through his shoes down to the bone in his foot. Most of his arm had been eaten away as well.

The Collyer Brothers' Legacy

Over 100 tons of the Collyers' stuff had been removed and much was stored in a seventh floor loft on William Street. Here the City held several auctions for the hermits' "treasures."

There was a separate sale for just the eleven pianos that were found in their house.

TWO MONTHS AFTER LANGLEY COLLYER WAS BURIED, ON JUNE 10, 1947, THE CITY AUCTIONED OFF 150 OF THE BROTHERS' RELICS. ONE OF THE 200 BIDDERS SPENT $300 ON STUFF. HE WAS MAX SCHAFFER, OWNER OF HUBERT'S MUSEUM AND FLEA CIRCUS ON 42nd STREET.

HOMER CARVED HIS INITIALS ON THIS OLD DESK.

ONE MAN MADE AN UNUSUAL OFFER...

I'D LIKE TO BUY THE COLLYER HOUSE AND TURN IT INTO A MYSTERY MUSEUM AND CHARGE ADMISSION.

BUT SUPREME COURT JUSTICE EDWARD LUMBARD MADE THE FINAL RULING.

THE COLLYER HOUSE IS UNSAFE AND MUST BE TORN DOWN!

THE PLACE WAS RAZED IN 1948.

MEANTIME, PEOPLE FROM CANADA TO BRAZIL WERE CLAIMING TO BE HEIRS. IT TOOK OVER THREE YEARS TO VERIFY ABOUT TWENTY LEGITIMATE CLAIMANTS.

LASTLY, THE COLLYERS SPAWNED AN EXPRESSION THAT WAS USED BY MANY PARENTS IN NEW YORK IN THE LATE 1940's.

YOUR ROOM'S A MESS! WHAT'RE YA TRYIN' TO BE, ONE OF THE COLLYER BROTHERS?

BROOKLYN DODGERS

Soon after the Collyer mansion was torn down, Mrs. Beatrice Lewis of 8 West 128th Street took it upon herself to keep the lot clean. She stuck to that task for over a dozen years.

In 1955 she organized over a dozen youngsters from the neighborhood to plant flowers on the property.

This is a story about a mild-mannered, ex-janitor who turned to counterfeiting simply because it was the easiest way to "make" the little money he needed to keep up his modest way of life.

READY CASH

An aide to the chief of the Secret Service explained, "...the fact that Miuller was a small operator made him all the harder to catch. He was a nuisance, not because of the amount of money involved, but because he had persisted so long."

BORN 1876 IN AUSTRIA, EMERICH JUETTNER CAME TO NEW YORK AT AGE 14 AND GOT A JOB GILDING FRAMES. SOMEWHERE ALONG THE LINE HE CHANGED HIS NAME TO **EDWARD MIULLER.**

AROUND 1932 MIULLER MOVED INTO A 2 ROOM, 5th FLOOR APARTMENT AT 204 W. 96 ST.

WHILE THE DEPRESSION DRAGGED ON, MIULLER WAS NEVER SHORT OF CASH. HE CLAIMED,

I COLLECT AND SELL JUNK.

ACTUALLY, HE **MADE** JUST ENOUGH MONEY TO GET BY, AND THAT WAS HIS SECRET. OL'EDWARD PRINTED COUNTERFEIT BILLS ON ORDINARY TABLET PAPER.

MIULLER PASSED HIS BOGUS BUCKS IN SUBWAYS, STORES, & TAVERNS ON THE WEST SIDE FROM 72nd TO 116th STREET AT THE RATE OF $12 TO $15 PER WEEK.

HE COUNTERFEITED **ONE DOLLAR BILLS,** PROBABLY THE WORST EVER MADE, AS THEY HAD A MISSPELLING.

DESPITE MR. MIULLER'S SHORTCOMINGS, THE U.S. SECRET SERVICE WAS UNABLE TO FIND HIM FOR **16 YEARS.**

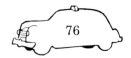

A week before Miuller's arrest, an Associated Press item appeared in New York newspapers referring to the recent upsurge in counterfeiting. Secret Service Chief James J. Maloney commented that one of their biggest headaches was trying to capture the small-time operator in New York who manufactured and distributed one dollar bills.

MISTER 880

It did not take an expert to spot Miuller's phony bills. The paper felt different, the printing was smudged, and his spelling was awful.

AT 5 A.M., DEC. 4, 1947 EDWARD MIULLER WAS AWAKENED BY HIS DOG'S BARKING.

HIS APARTMENT AT 204 W. 96th ST. WAS ON FIRE. HE ESCAPED UNHURT.

AFTERWARDS, THE FIREMEN TOSSED JUNK FROM MIULLER'S PLACE INTO THE ALLEY.

A FEW DAYS LATER, A SNOW-STORM COVERED THE JUNK PILE.

A JANUARY THAW MELTED THE SNOW. KIDS STARTED TO PLAY ON THE HEAP OF JUNK.

WHAT'S THIS?

THEY'RE PLATES FOR MAKING PHONY DOUGH.

LET'S GO TO THE COPS!

THEY TOOK THE PLATES TO DETECTIVES LOUIS BEHRENS AND JOHN NORTH AT THE WEST 100th ST. POLICE STATION.

SECRET SERVICE AGENTS SAM CALLAHAN AND TOM BURKE WERE NOTIFIED.

WE FINALLY GOT A BREAK ON CASE 880!

ON JAN. 14, 1948 THEY ARRESTED 72-YEAR-OLD MIULLER AT HIS DAUGHTER'S HOUSE IN FLUSHING.

OVER A 16 YEAR PERIOD, MIULLER MADE & SPENT $5,000 IN BOGUS $1 BILLS.

MR. MIULLER WAS SENTENCED TO A YEAR AND A DAY IN JAIL, AND FINED ONE DOLLAR... IN REAL MONEY.

HOLLYWOOD MADE MIULLER A NATIONAL CELEBRITY IN 1950 WHEN EDMUND GWENN PORTRAYED HIM IN THE MOVIE CALLED "MR. 880."

A Brief History of Sports in the Big Apple

Alexander Joy Cartwright, Jr. was born on April 17, 1820 in New York City, the oldest of seven children. Besides sports, he had a life-long interest in fire-fighting and served at various times as a volunteer fireman. One of his brothers, Benjamin, became one of New York City's first fire commissioners.

The Man Who Invented Baseball

AT THE AGE OF 22, IN 1842, **ALEXANDER** (ALICK) **CARTWRIGHT** GOT A JOB AS A TELLER AT THE UNION BANK IN NEW YORK CITY.

THE BANK BURNED DOWN IN 1845, SO ALICK & HIS BROTHER, ALFRED, OPENED A BOOK & STATIONERY SHOP ON WALL STREET.

ON WEEKENDS, ALICK ORGANIZED SPORTING EVENTS FOR HIS WALL STREET BUDDIES.

THEY USUALLY PLAYED IN A PARK AT 27th ST. & 4th AVE.

AT THE TIME THERE WAS A LOT OF ANTI-BRITISH SENTIMENT IN THE COUNTRY.

WE REFUSE TO PLAY BRITISH GAMES LIKE CRICKET!

THIS PROMPTED ALICK TO DRAFT A SET OF RULES FOR A NEW GAME...

9 PLAYERS...3 BASES...3 STRIKES AND YOU'RE OUT... 3 OUTS PER INNING. 90 FT. BETWEEN BASES...

ONE DAY IN 1845, CARTWRIGHT WENT TO A FIELD ON MURRAY HILL OFF 3rd AVE. WITH HIS SET OF RULES.

HE LAID OUT A DIAMOND-SHAPED FIELD WITH 3 SAND-FILLED BAGS FOR BASES AND AN IRON PLATE FOR HOME BASE.

AT FIRST THEY RIDICULED CARTWRIGHT'S IDEA. THEN, TO HUMOR HIM, HIS FRIENDS CONSENTED TO PLAY HIS NEW GAME, AND THE AMERICAN PASTIME WAS BORN!

78

At first, baseball was a "gentleman's game," and the Knickerbocker Club insisted on high standards of moral conduct and fair play. The Knickerbockers had 28 players in their first game in 1845 and Cartwright was a pitcher.

The Knickerbockers

The Knickerbockers played 14 recorded games in Hoboken, NJ in 1845 and Cartwright's team appeared to have lost more than it won.

A FEW WEEKS AFTER HE INVENTED THE GAME OF BASEBALL, ALEXANDER CARTWRIGHT ORGANIZED THE WORLD'S **FIRST FORMAL BASEBALL CLUB** ON SEPTEMBER 23, 1845.

HE NAMED IT AFTER A DEFUNCT **FIRE COMPANY** OF WHICH HE HAD BEEN A MEMBER, THE KNICKERBOCKERS.

THE CLUB OBTAINED THEIR OWN UNIFORMS AND PLAYED AMONG THEMSELVES ON ELYSIAN FIELDS IN **HOBOKEN, NEW JERSEY.**

ON JUNE 19, 1846, THE KNICKS CHALLENGED THE *NEW YORK CLUB* TO A BASEBALL GAME.

THE LOSER PAYS FOR A BANQUET AT McCARTY'S HOTEL IN HOBOKEN.

THE KNICKS WERE BEATEN IN THEIR FIRST INTER-CLUB GAME, 23-1. THE *NEW YORK CLUB* NEVER PLAYED THE KNICKERBOCKERS AGAIN.

THE KNICKS GREW TO ABOUT FIFTY MEMBERS AND REMAINED AS AN AMATEUR CLUB UNTIL IT DISBANDED IN THE EARLY 1870'S.

ON MARCH 1, 1849 CARTWRIGHT LEFT NEW YORK FOR GOOD, TAKING HIS FAMILY TO THE GOLD RUSH IN CALIFORNIA.

WHENEVER THE WAGON TRAIN STOPPED, CARTWRIGHT ORGANIZED A BALL GAME. THUS, HE INTRODUCED BASEBALL ACROSS THE COUNTRY TO SUCH CITIES AS PITTSBURGH, COLUMBUS, ST. LOUIS, KANSAS CITY, OAKLAND, & FINALLY SAN FRANCISCO.

Abner Doubleday was born June 26, 1819 in Ballston Spa, NY and graduated from the U. S. Military Academy in 1842. He served in both the Mexican and Civil Wars, and saw action at Chancellorsville, VA and Gettysburg, PA. After the Civil War, Doubleday stayed in the regular army as a colonel. While on duty in San Francisco, CA (1869-71), he secured the charter for the city's first cable-car railway. He died on January 26, 1893.

The Abner Doubleday Myth

AROUND 1905, SPORTING GOODS MANUFACTURER ALBERT GOODWILL SPALDING FORMED A COMMITTEE OF SEVEN POLITICIANS AND CRONIES TO FIND OUT WHO *REALLY* INVENTED BASEBALL.

SINCE NONE OF THEM KNEW HOW TO DO SCHOLARLY RESEARCH, THEY COLLECTED A LOT OF UNPROVEN STORIES.

IN 1907 SPALDING RECEIVED A LETTER POSTMARKED DENVER, COLORADO...

FROM AN 80 YEAR-OLD RETIRED MINING ENGINEER, ABNER GRAVES.

GRAVES REPORTED THAT IN 1839 ABNER DOUBLEDAY LAID OUT A *DIAMOND* FIELD AND STARTED THE GAME OF **BASEBALL** BEHIND A TAILOR SHOP IN COOPERSTOWN, NY.

SPALDING BELIEVED IT AND REPORTED TO THE COMMITTEE,

IT CERTAINLY APPEALS TO AMERICAN PRIDE TO HAVE HAD THE NATIONAL GAME CREATED AND NAMED BY A MAJOR GENERAL IN THE U.S. ARMY!

HOWEVER, SPALDING'S COMMITTEE NEVER QUESTIONED GRAVES' MEMORY. NOR DID THEY READ ANY OF DOUBLEDAY'S WRITINGS WHICH NEVER MENTIONED BASEBALL.

DOUBLEDAY COULD NOT HAVE BEEN IN COOPERSTOWN IN 1839 BECAUSE HE WAS A CADET AT WEST POINT, AND THE ACADEMY DID NOT GIVE HIM LEAVE THAT YEAR.

BY THE WAY... THERE IS A "FIRST" THAT IS ATTRIBUTED TO DOUBLEDAY. DURING THE LEAD-OFF BATTLE OF THE CIVIL WAR, HE GAVE THE FIRST ORDER TO THE UNION TROOPS IN FORT SUMTER TO RETURN FIRE ON THE CONFEDERATES.

No sportswriter has ever approached the quantity of Henry Chadwick's work. Besides numerous books on baseball, he wrote how-to booklets on cricket, handball, and (his other passion) chess. Chadwick penned all of his material in a handsome longhand. He never used a typewriter.

The Reluctant "Father of Baseball"

HENRY CHADWICK WAS BORN OCT. 6, 1824 IN ENGLAND AND CAME TO BROOKLYN IN 1837 WHERE HE LIVED THE REST OF HIS LIFE.

HE SOLD STORIES TO THE LONG ISLAND *STAR* AT 19. FOUR YEARS LATER HE SAW HIS FIRST BASEBALL GAME WITH HIS BRIDE AT ELYSIAN FIELDS IN HOBOKEN, N.J.

JOINING THE NEW YORK *CLIPPER* IN 1858 HE WROTE ONLY ABOUT BASEBALL. FOR THE NEXT HALF-CENTURY HE COVERED THE GAME FOR THE BIGGEST MAGAZINES AND NEWSPAPERS IN THE COUNTRY.

HE COMPILED THE FIRST RULE BOOK IN 1859. DURING GAMES HE ATTENDED, UMPIRES OFTEN STOPPED PLAY TO ASK HIS INTERPRETATION OF A RULE.

CHADWICK WROTE THE FIRST "HOW-TO" BOOKS FOR BOYS AND GIRLS.

HE PUBLISHED THE FIRST LIST OF PROFESSIONAL BASEBALL PLAYERS IN 1872. IT CONTAINED THEIR BIRTH DATES, HOME TOWNS, HEIGHTS & WEIGHTS — A FORM STILL SEEN IN MODERN ROSTERS.

HE INVENTED THE SCORING AND BOX SCORE SYSTEMS.

ON CHADWICK'S 80th BIRTHDAY IN 1904, PRES. TEDDY ROOSEVELT CALLED HIM THE "FATHER OF BASEBALL." CHADWICK HATED THE NICKNAME, CLAIMING "BASEBALL HAS NO FATHER."

MR. CHADWICK DIED IN BROOKLYN ON APR. 20, 1908. FLAGS AT ALL BALL PARKS WERE FLOWN AT HALF-MAST. HIS LONGTIME FRIEND, AL SPALDING, PAID FOR HIS TOMBSTONE IN GREENWOOD CEMETERY, BROOKLYN.

IN 1938 HENRY CHADWICK BECAME THE ONLY PROFESSIONAL SPORTSWRITER EVER ENSHRINED IN THE BASEBALL HALL OF FAME.

Big Apple Almanac by Patrick M. Reynolds

PAY BALL

PLAYING A SPORT FOR MONEY WAS CONSIDERED REPULSIVE BY AMERICAN FANS IN THE MID 1800'S. THEN, BASEBALL BECAME VERY POPULAR.

A FEW BASEBALL CLUBS DECIDED TO CASH IN ON THIS POPULARITY. DURING THE CIVIL WAR THE **BROOKLYN** *ATLANTICS* STARTED TO CHARGE ADMISSION TO THEIR GAMES.

AFTERWARDS, THE PLAYERS DIVIDED THE RECEIPTS AMONG THEMSELVES. OTHER CLUBS DISGUISED THEIR PAYROLLS.

FOR EXAMPLE, TAMMANY HALL'S "BOSS" TWEED, PRESIDENT OF THE **NEW YORK** *MUTUALS* FROM 1860 TO 1871, CLASSIFIED HIS PLAYERS AS SWEEPERS AND CLERKS ON THE NEW YORK CITY PAYROLL.

IT COST THE TAXPAYERS **$30,000** A YEAR.

BY 1870 THERE WERE PROFESSIONALS ON MOST OF THE LEADING TEAMS SUCH AS THE TROY (NY) *HAYMAKERS*, THE BROOKLYN *ATLANTICS*, THE *MUTUALS*, THE CHICAGO *WHITE STOCKINGS*, THE LANDISBURGH (NY) *UNIONS*, THE CINCINNATI *BUCKEYES*, AND THE BALTIMORE *MARYLANDERS*.

Al Reach was president of the Philadelphia Phillies from 1883 to 1902. During that time, his sporting goods company got the contract to produce the official ball for the rival American Baseball League.

The First Professional Baseball Player

IN THE BEGINNING, BASEBALL WAS AN EXCLUSIVELY AMATEUR SPORT.

ONE OF THE BEST SLUGGERS WAS ALFRED J. REACH FROM LONDON, ENGLAND WHO PLAYED FOR THE BROOKLYN ATLANTICS.

IN 1864 THE PHILADELPHIA ATHLETICS OFFERED AL REACH $25 A WEEK AS "EXPENSES," MAKING THE SECOND BASEMAN THE FIRST PROFESSIONAL BASEBALL PLAYER.

THE FANS HATED THE IDEA OF PLAY FOR PAY. NEVERTHELESS, AL REACH AND THE A'S ROLLED UP SCORES LIKE 101-8 AND 162-14.

THE BROOKLYN ATLANTICS CHALLENGED THE ATHLETICS TO A *GREAT GAME* FOR THE U.S. CHAMPIONSHIP ON OCT. 1, 1866.

THIRTY THOUSAND FANS PAID FROM $5 TO $25 FOR ADMISSION.

HOWEVER, THE OVERFLOWING CROWD SPILLED ONTO THE FIELD AND THE GAME WAS CALLED IN THE FOURTH INNING.

AFTER LEAVING THE A'S IN 1876, REACH STARTED A SPORTING GOODS MANUFACTURING COMPANY.

HE DIED A MULTI MILLIONAIRE IN ATLANTIC CITY, NJ ON JAN. 14, 1928.

The ball club owners elected Morgan G. Bulkeley to be the first president of the National League. He was a banker, president of the Hartford (CT) Club, and Chairman of the Aetna Life Insurance Company.

 # The National League

Morgan Bulkeley quit as president of the National League after one year to enter politics and was subsequently elected governor of Connecticut. He is now a member of the Baseball Hall of Fame in Cooperstown, NY.

WHEN BASEBALL CLUBS STARTED PAYING THEIR PLAYERS A SALARY, THEY FORMED THE NATIONAL ASSOCIATION OF BASE BALL PLAYERS, BUT IT HAD NO CLOUT. FOR EXAMPLE, TEAMS OFTEN DID NOT SHOW UP FOR GAMES.

PLAYERS SWITCHED TEAMS WHENEVER THEY WISHED.

THE SILK-HATTED UMPIRES, USUALLY UNPAID AND UNPROFESSIONAL, OFTEN LOST CONTROL OF THE GAMES.

"BOSS" TWEED, PRESIDENT OF THE NEW YORK MUTUALS, WAS KNOWN TO HAVE FIXED GAMES.

ENOUGH WAS ENOUGH. THE OWNERS MET IN 1876 AT THE GRAND UNION HOTEL ON PARK AVE. & 42nd ST., AND ORGANIZED **THE NATIONAL LEAGUE OF PROFESSIONAL BASE BALL CLUBS.**

THE NATIONAL LEAGUE SET ADMISSION PRICES, PAID UMPIRES, AND, IN A BID FOR RESPECTABILITY, BANNED GAMBLING AND GAMES ON SUNDAY.

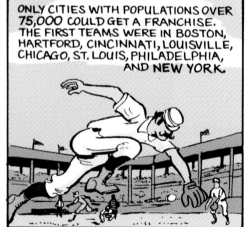

ONLY CITIES WITH POPULATIONS OVER 75,000 COULD GET A FRANCHISE. THE FIRST TEAMS WERE IN BOSTON, HARTFORD, CINCINNATI, LOUISVILLE, CHICAGO, ST. LOUIS, PHILADELPHIA, AND NEW YORK.

When the National Baseball League was organized in 1876, the New York *Mutuals* was a charter member. However, the team was a New York club in name only because it played its games at the Union Grounds in Brooklyn.

The First Mets

Before the 1876 season was over, the New York *Mutuals* was thrown out of the league after its players refused to go on the road.

JOHN B. DAY WAS A WEALTHY MANUFACTURER WHOSE FACTORY WAS ON MANHATTAN'S LOWER EAST SIDE.

IN 1881 HE PUT TOGETHER A PROFESSIONAL BASEBALL CLUB WHICH HE DUBBED THE METROPOLITANS OR **METS.**

THE METS OPERATED AS AN INDEPENDENT CLUB THAT YEAR, MEANING THEY WERE NOT PART OF A LEAGUE.

THEIR STAR PITCHER, **HUGH DAILY,** WON 38 GAMES, DESPITE HAVING LOST AN ARM WHEN HE WAS A CHILD.

IN 1882, THE METS ENTERED THE AMERICAN ASSOCIATION. THE BROOKLYN *ATLANTICS* WERE ALREADY IN THE ASSOCIATION, BUT BROOKLYN WAS A SEPARATE CITY AT THE TIME. THEREFORE, THE METS WERE NEW YORK CITY'S **FIRST MAJOR LEAGUE TEAM.**

Between 1877 and 1890, twenty-three cities including Worcester, Indianapolis, Buffalo, Troy, Syracuse, and Providence fielded teams in the National League. During that period, most of the clubs folded, while only Boston and Chicago endured without missing a single season.

JOHN B. DAY'S BALL CLUB, THE NEW YORK METS, WON THE AMERICAN ASSOCIATION'S PENNANT IN 1884.

THEY FACED THE NATIONAL LEAGUE CHAMPIONS, THE PROVIDENCE (RHODE ISLAND) GRAYBEARDS IN WHAT COULD TECHNICALLY BE CALLED **THE FIRST WORLD SERIES.**

THE GRAYS SWEPT THE "SERIES" IN THREE STRAIGHT GAMES.

A YEAR EARLIER,

IN 1883, JOHN DAY PURCHASED THE TROY HAYMAKERS AND BROUGHT THEM TO MANHATTAN. HE KEPT THE BEST PLAYERS FROM TROY INCLUDING (FROM LEFT) WILLIAM "BUCK" EWING, THE GREATEST PLAYER AT THE TIME; JOHN MONTGOMERY WARD; MICKEY WELCH; AND ROGER CONNOR.

FOR A WHILE, THE TEAM WAS SIMPLY KNOWN AS

THE NEW YORKS.

In 1848 four Brothers of the Christian Schools kicked off the order's work in the United States by setting up St. Vincent's Acacemy on Canal Street, New York City. The School was moved on May 13, 1853 to a new site on 131st Street and Broadway in the Manhattanville section of the city. The name was changed to the Academy of the Holy Infancy.

BROTHER JASPER

THE ACADEMY OF THE HOLY INFANCY BECAME **MANHATTAN COLLEGE** IN 1863.

FOR THE NEXT THREE DECADES ITS PREFECT OF DISCIPLINE AND MOST DYNAMIC PROFESSOR WAS A MAN FROM KILKENNY, IRELAND NAMED **BROTHER JASPER OF MARY.**

THE BROTHERS OF CHRISTIAN SCHOOLS FOUNDED THE COLLEGE.

BROTHER JASPER ORGANIZED THE SCHOOL'S FIRST LITERARY SOCIETY AND STARTED ITS FIRST BAND. HE ALSO INVENTED A TRADITION THAT EXISTS THROUGHOUT THE WORLD TODAY.

IN JUNE, 1882, MANHATTAN COLLEGE WAS PLAYING BASEBALL AGAINST THE SEMI-PRO METROPOLITANS AT 161st STREET. JASPER, WHO WAS ALSO THE COLLEGE'S FIRST ATHLETIC DIRECTOR, NOTICED THAT THE FANS WERE GETTING FIDGETY.

AT BAT IS TIP O'NEILL OF THE METS.

SO, HE CALLED A TIME-OUT DURING THE 7th INNING. THE NEW YORK *GIANTS* DID THE SAME WHEN THEY PLAYED THE COLLEGE A FEW DAYS LATER. THUS BEGAN **THE 7th INNING STRETCH.**

MANHATTAN COLLEGE IS NOW IN THE BRONX AND ITS TEAMS ARE CALLED **THE JASPERS!**

88

Charles H. Byrne made his fortune in real estate, then purchased the Brooklyn Superbas in 1883. As members of the Interstate Base-ball League, they won the pennant that year. The following season, Byrne moved his team to a higher class--the American Association. In 1890 he put the Superbas in the National League.

The Brooklyn Dodgers

CHARLES EBBETS STARTED TO WORK FOR THE SUPERBAS IN 1883 AS A PEANUT VENDOR AND TICKET SELLER.

HARRY **VON DER HORST,** THE TEAM'S OWNER, FIGURED EBBETS WOULD WORK HARDER IF HE HAD A PIECE OF THE ACTION SO HE SOLD CHARLIE SOME OF HIS SHARES.

VAN DER HORST'S HEALTH HIT THE SKIDS IN 1902 & HE DECIDED TO SELL HIS STOCK.

NED HANLON, THE SUPERBAS' **MANAGER,** ANNOUNCED:

I INTEND TO **BUY** THE TEAM AND MOVE IT TO **BALTIMORE.**

EBBETS WANTED TO KEEP THE TEAM IN BROOKLYN. FOR THE NEXT 3 YEARS HE SCOURED THE BOROUGH FOR BACKERS TO HELP HIM BUY THE SUPERBAS.

ALONG CAME HENRY **MEDICUS,** A FURNITURE DEALER WHO HAD MORE FAITH IN EBBETS THAN HANLON. MEDICUS LOANED CHARLIE THE AMOUNT HE NEEDED.

THAT SEASON, **1905,** THE SUPERBAS SLUMPED INTO THE CELLAR OF THE STANDINGS AND HANLON WAS CANNED.

TO GET TO THE BALL PARK FANS HAD TO CROSS A BUSY INTERSECTION BY DODGING TROLLEY CARS. THIS PROMPTED MR. EBBETS IN 1906 TO RENAME HIS TEAM THE BROOKLYN **DODGERS.**

Ebbets almost went broke bringing his dream of a new ballpark to a reality. He had to sell half of his interest in the team to Edward and Stephen McKeever, two brothers who had made a bundle in the construciton business.

From Pigpen To Bull Pen

WHEN CHARLIE **EBBETS** TOOK OVER THE OLD BROOKLYN SUPERBAS IN 1905 AND CHANGED THEIR NAME TO THE **DODGERS** THE TEAM WAS PLAYING IN **WASHINGTON PARK** IN THE HEIGHTS.

EBBETS WANTED A LARGER STADIUM. HE TOOK WALKS THRU THE BOROUGH EVERY DAY LOOKING FOR A SITE TO BUILD ONE.

IN FLATBUSH HE WANDERED INTO A PUTRID 4½ ACRE SLUM WITH A HUGE GARBAGE PIT IN THE CENTER. FARMERS BROUGHT THEIR PIGS TO FEED AT THIS PIT; HENCE THE NAME **PIGTOWN**. EBBETS THOUGHT...

A **PERFECT** PLACE FOR THE DODGERS TO PLAY!

EBBETS FOUND **40 OWNERS** OF THE LAND IN PIGTOWN. HE FORMED A CORPORATION AND BOUGHT THE FIRST PARCEL IN 1908. IT TOOK THREE YEARS TO BUY THE REST...

...EXCEPT FOR ONE SMALL PARCEL. HE TRACKED DOWN THE OWNER, FIRST TO CALIFORNIA, THEN BERLIN, PARIS AND...

...FINALLY, MONTCLAIR, NEW JERSEY. THE GUY **FORGOT** HE OWNED THE PLOT BUT SOLD IT TO EBBETS FOR **$500**.

ON MARCH 4, 1912 MR. EBBETS BROKE GROUND FOR HIS STADIUM. A YEAR LATER PIGTOWN WAS TRANSFORMED INTO THE 32,111 SEAT **EBBETS FIELD**.

Ebbets Field finally opened on April 5, 1913 with a 3-2 Brooklyn victory over their arch-rivals, the New York Giants.

Professional ball players first got organized in 1867 through the National Association of Base Ball Players. This group prohibited not only integrated teams, but any African-American pro baseball team. It was not until the formation of the Negro National League in 1920 that black players could make money in America's pastime. At the time, Jackie Robinson was a year old.

JACKIE WAS NOT THE FIRST

WHEN JACKIE **ROBINSON** SIGNED WITH THE BROOKLYN *DODGERS* IN 1947 HE BECAME THE FIRST AFRICAN-AMERICAN IN THE MAJOR LEAGUES.

NOT SO!

JOHN W. **"BUD" FOWLER** OF COOPERSTOWN, NEW YORK PLAYED FOR A MINOR LEAGUE TEAM IN NEW CASTLE, PA IN 1877 MAKING HIM THE **FIRST BLACK PROFESSIONAL BASEBALL PLAYER.**

FOR THE NEXT 25 YEARS, BUD BARNSTORMED AROUND THE COUNTRY, FROM MASSACHUSETTS TO COLORADO, PLAYING WHEREEVER BLACK PLAYERS WERE PERMITTED.

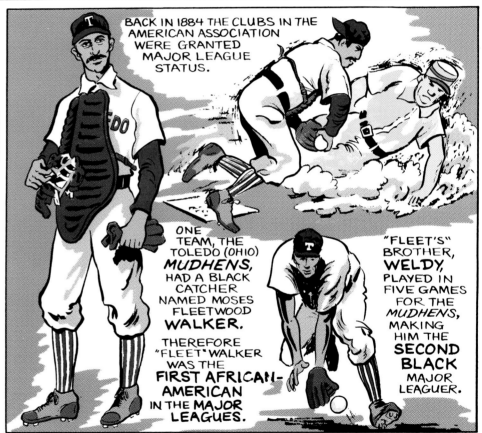

BACK IN 1884 THE CLUBS IN THE AMERICAN ASSOCIATION WERE GRANTED MAJOR LEAGUE STATUS.

ONE TEAM, THE TOLEDO (OHIO) **MUDHENS,** HAD A BLACK CATCHER NAMED MOSES FLEETWOOD **WALKER.**

THEREFORE "FLEET" WALKER WAS THE **FIRST AFRICAN-AMERICAN** IN THE MAJOR LEAGUES.

"FLEET'S" BROTHER, **WELDY,** PLAYED IN FIVE GAMES FOR THE *MUDHENS,* MAKING HIM THE **SECOND BLACK** MAJOR LEAGUER.

Guttfried "Dutch Fred" Walbaum owned the Guttenberg Race Track in New Jersey where the results of many races were known before they started. In 1890 he acquired a 90 percent of the Saratoga track for the tidy sum of $375,000. Frank Farrell had his fingers in a number of questionably legal pies, but was most famous as a race track plunger (a reckless bettor or speculator).

THE CASINO

THEY CONTACTED THE COUNTRY'S LEADING ARCHITECT AT THE TIME, **STANFORD WHITE,** AND GAVE HIM **A HALF MILLION DOLLARS** TO TURN THE PLACE INTO A HIGH CLASS GAMBLING EMPORIUM.

WHITE SPENT THE MONEY IN EUROPE ON OIL PAINTINGS, VELVET CARPETS, PERSIAN RUGS, AND OTHER OBJECTS D'ART.

AROUND 1893 MESSRS. WALBAUM (LEFT) AND FARRELL (RIGHT) TEAMED UP AND BOUGHT A HOUSE AT 33 WEST 33rd STREET.

AT THE DOGE'S PALACE IN VENICE, ITALY, HE PAID $60,000 FOR THE SECOND FLOOR BANISTER WHICH TOOK TEN MASTER CRAFTSMEN TWO YEARS TO CARVE, AND...

IN THE DOGE'S WINE CELLAR WAS AN INTRICATELY WROUGHT BRONZE DOOR SWINGING THERE SINCE 1498. WHITE BOUGHT IT FOR $20,000.

THE ARCHITECT SHIPPED THESE RENAISSANCE TREASURES TO AMERICA AND INSTALLED THEM IN NEW YORK'S CLASSIEST GAMBLING CASINO, *THE HOUSE WITH THE BRONZE DOOR.*

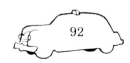

One of the esteemed patrons of the Farrell-Walbaum establishment was "Lucky" Baldwin of California where he ran a hotel and a gambling emporium. He also operated one of the largest thoroughbred breeding farms at the time. That farm became the site of the Santa Anita race track.

THE BRONZE DOOR

Another Bronze Door regular was George E. Smith, better known as "Pittsburgh Phil," one of the smartest and richest horse bettors in the history of the sport.

FROM 1895 TO 1902 THE MOST POPULAR GAMBLING JOINT AMONG NEW YORK'S RICH CROWD WAS LOCATED A FEW STEPS WEST OF THE WALDORF HOTEL ON 33rd STREET. FOLKS CALLED IT *THE HOUSE WITH THE BRONZE DOOR* BECAUSE OF THE HUGE ITALIAN RENAISSANCE DOOR AT THE REAR OF THE ENTRANCE HALL.

BEHIND THE DOOR WAS THE CASINO WHERE AT LEAST $50,000 EXCHANGED HANDS EVERY NIGHT. SOME OF ITS REGULAR HIGH ROLLERS INCLUDED "DIAMOND JIM" BRADY, LILLIAN RUSSELL, "REGGIE" VANDERBILT, AND JAMES GORDON BENNETT, JR.

THE OWNERS, FRANK FARRELL AND "DUTCH FRED" WALBAUM, SPENT OVER $25,000 A YEAR ON FOOD, FINE CIGARS, WINES, AND LIQUORS WHICH WERE AVAILABLE FREE TO THEIR PATRONS.

Despite anti-gambling laws, New York was a wide-open town in the late 1890's. Nevertheless...

casino owners always had to be on their guard against anti-gambling groups and reform-minded district attorneys.

THE RAID

THE BRONZE DOOR PROVED TO BE AN EFFECTIVE DEFENSE AGAINST THESE "DO-GOODERS."

ONE NIGHT, ASS'T. DISTRICT ATTORNEY WM. T. JEROME LED A RAID AGAINST THE PLACE. THE DOOR WITHSTOOD BLOWTORCHES.

MEANWHILE, GAMBLING PARAPHERNALIA AND PATRONS, INCLUDING "DIAMOND JIM" BRADY, WERE ESCORTED OUT THROUGH A SECRET PASSAGE, OVER ROOFTOPS TO A HOUSE DOWN THE STREET.

ANOTHER GET-AWAY ROUTE WAS THROUGH A TUNNEL INTO THE HOUSE NEXT DOOR, ALSO OWNED BY THE PROPRIETORS OF THE HOUSE WITH THE BRONZE DOOR.

94

Meanwhile, in another part of the country...A former sportswriter from Cincinnati named Byron Bancroft Johnson reorganized the Western (Baseball) Association and announced it would take the field in 1900 as the American League.

Johnson placed teams in several big eastern cities to compete directly with the National League. They included: Cleveland, Chicago, Washington, Philadelphia, Boston, and Baltimore.

BESIDES BEING A PART OWNER OF *THE HOUSE WITH THE BRONZE DOOR* GAMBLING PARLOR, FRANK FARRELL HAD A CHAIN OF ABOUT 250 POOL ROOMS ALL OVER NEW YORK CITY. HE WAS A CLOSE PAL OF POLICE CHIEF "BIG BILL" DEVERY, PROBABLY THE MOST CORRUPT COP IN THE HISTORY OF THE BIG APPLE.

The "Burglars" Ball Club

Eager to lure fans away from the New York *Giants*, Johnson was willing to sell the Baltimore franchise to anyone who could come up with the cash. The buyers were none other than Farrell & Devery.

IN 1903 FARRELL AND DEVERY PURCHASED AN AMERICAN LEAGUE CLUB IN BALTIMORE AND MOVED IT TO THE BIG APPLE. THE NEW OWNERS' REPUTATION PROMPTED THE FANS TO CALL THE TEAM THE "BURGLARS." ONE OF THE WORST TEAMS IN BASEBALL HISTORY THE "BURGLARS" MANAGED TO PLACE SECOND IN 1912.

FINALLY, IN 1914, THEY SOLD THE TEAM TO JACOB RUPPERT AND TILLINGHAST HUSTON FOR $460,000 GIVING THEM A PROFIT OF 2,500 PERCENT OF THE ORIGINAL PRICE OF $18,000.

STANDING ON THE SITE OF FARRELL'S *HOUSE WITH THE BRONZE DOOR* IS THE EMPIRE STATE BUILDING

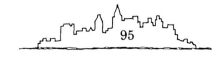

By the way, here are a few more details on the "Burglars" ball club.

THE NEW YORK GIANTS KEPT THE AMERICAN LEAGUE OUT OF THE CITY BY OUTBIDDING THEM ON BALLPARK SITES. BUT, IN 1903, "BIG BILL" DEVERY AND FRANK FARRELL PURCHASED A BASEBALL CLUB AND BUILT *HILLTOP PARK* AT 168th ST. & BROADWAY. SINCE THIS IS ONE OF THE HIGHEST POINTS ON MANHATTAN, THEY CALLED THEIR TEAM

the New York Highlanders.

FRANK FARRELL HAD BEEN A BARTENDER, A GAMBLING HOUSE OWNER, AND RACETRACK PLUNGER.

"BIG BILL" DEVERY, A RETIRED **POLICE COMMISSIONER,** NOW DABBLED IN REAL ESTATE.

THE HIGHLANDERS CAME FROM BALTIMORE. DEVERY AND FARRELL PAID **$18,000** FOR THE FRANCHISE AND MOVED IT TO NEW YORK.

SPORTS EDITORS WENT NUTS TRYING TO FIT THE NAME "HIGHLANDERS" INTO THE TRADITIONAL ONE-COLUMN SPACE.

BY 1913, SEVERAL SPORTSWRITERS: JIM PRICE OF THE NY PRESS, MARK ROTH OF THE GLOBE, AND SAM CRANE OF THE JOURNAL, WERE CLAIMING CREDIT FOR GIVING THE HIGH-LANDERS A **SHORTER NAME...**

THE NEW YORK YANKEES!

Another reason given for the name *Highlanders* was that the club's first president was Joseph W. Gordon, whose name suggested the Gordon Highlanders, a famous Scottish regiment.

Jack Norworth's hobby was collecting miniatures. His collection of about 25,000 items* was one of the largest in the country. It included tiny houses, books, a coach carved from a peach stone, a 3/4 inch long cannon that worked, and a one-inch square motion picture camera that filmed real movies.

JACK NORWORTH (1879-1959) OF **BROOKLYN** WAS A SONG AND DANCE MAN IN VAUDEVILLE AT THE TURN OF THE CENTURY.

ONE DAY IN 1908 NORWORTH WAS ON A SUBWAY WHEN HE NOTICED AN AD FOR THE NEW YORK GIANTS BASEBALL TEAM. HE GRABBED A SCRAP OF PAPER AND BEGAN SCRIBBLING.

A HALF-HOUR LATER HE HAD WRITTEN A SONG,

Take Me Out To The Ball Game.

NORWORTH ALSO PENNED *MEET ME IN APPLE BLOSSOM TIME.* IN ALL, HE COMPOSED ABOUT 3,000 SONGS, MANY FOR THE ZIEGFELD FOLLIES.

HE MARRIED **NORA BAYES,*** A SINGING STAR, IN 1907. WHILE TRAVELING THE VAUDEVILLE CIRCUIT THEY WROTE *SHINE ON HARVEST MOON.* THEY DIVORCED IN 1913.

IN 1942, 34 YEARS AFTER HE WROTE *TAKE ME OUT TO THE BALL GAME,* NORWORTH ATTENDED HIS FIRST BASEBALL GAME.

*Nora's real name was Dora Goldberg. Born in 1880, her big break in vaudeville came in 1902 when she sang *Down Where the Wurzburger Flows* at the Orpheum Theater in Brooklyn. For years afterwards, she was known as "The Wurzburger Girl." Miss Bayes died in 1928.

The World Series of Football

This could be considered the first Super Bowl.

PROFESSIONAL FOOTBALL WAS STILL IN ITS INFANCY AT THE TURN OF THE CENTURY, AND MOST OF THE TEAMS WERE IN SMALL CITIES AND TOWNS. IN DECEMBER, 1902...

TOM O'ROURKE, THE MANAGER OF MADISON SQUARE GARDEN, FIGURED HE COULD BOOST THE GARDEN'S ATTENDANCE WITH A CHAMPIONSHIP PLAYOFF OF THE FIVE BEST FOOTBALL TEAMS IN THE COUNTRY.

IT'S CALLED **THE WORLD SERIES!**

THREE NATIONAL FOOTBALL LEAGUE TEAMS AND THE WATERTOWN (NEW YORK) RED AND BLACKS HAD THE BEST RECORDS, BUT EACH TURNED DOWN O'ROURKE'S OFFER.

SO O'ROURKE SETTLED FOR THE ORANGE (NEW JERSEY) TEAM, THREE CLUBS FROM NEW YORK— SYRACUSE, WARLOW, AND THE KNICKERBOCKERS—AND A SQUAD MADE UP OF PHILADELPHIA ATHLETICS AND PHILLIES FOOTBALL PLAYERS CALLED "NEW YORK."

THIS WAS THE FIRST TIME FOOTBALL WAS PLAYED INDOORS. SYRACUSE WON THREE STRAIGHT GAMES AND BECAME THE FIRST NATIONAL CHAMPIONS.

POST SCRIPT—THE FOLLOWING YEAR, THE PRO BASEBALL CLUBS "BORROWED" O'ROURKE'S IDEA AND HELD THE FIRST BASEBALL WORLD SERIES.

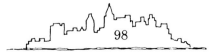

There are two versions of where the word "polo" originated. Some claim it was derived from the Tibetal *pulu* meaning willow, the tree from which the wood was taken to make the mallets and balls for the game. Others contend the word polo is a Balti term meaning "ball."

Emperor A-pao-chi of China was the all-time poor sport. In A.D. 910, his favorite player was killed during a polo match, so he promptly ordered the beheading of every surviving player.

CHUKKAR*

POLO GOES BACK OVER 2,000 YEARS WHEN IT WAS FIRST USED AS A GAME TO TRAIN CAVALRY UNITS IN PERSIA. AT TIMES THERE WERE A HUNDRED PLAYERS ON EACH SIDE.

MUSLIM CONQUERORS INTRODUCED THE GAME TO INDIA IN THE 13th CENTURY. THE BRITISH GOT HOOKED ON POLO WHEN THEY OCCUPIED THE COUNTRY 600 YEARS LATER.

JAMES GORDON BENNETT, THE PUBLISHER OF THE *NEW YORK TRIBUNE* AND WORLD RENOWNED PLAYBOY, SAW A MATCH AT HURLINGHAM, ENGLAND IN 1875 AND FELL IN LOVE WITH POLO.

A YEAR LATER, MR. BENNETT BROUGHT THE GAME TO THE UNITED STATES AND PLAYED THE FIRST MATCH IN NEW YORK CITY.

* BY THE WAY, A POLO MATCH CONSISTS OF SIX PERIODS OF 7½ MINUTES EACH, CALLED CHUKKARS-A HINDI WORD MEANING TURNS OR CIRCLES.

THE OPENING SERVE

The game of lawn tennis was invented by Major Walter Clopton Winfield in Nantclwyd, Wales.

MARY EWING **OUTERBRIDGE** INTRODUCED **TENNIS** TO THE UNITED STATES IN THE SPRING OF 1874.

SHE HAD PLAYED THE GAME WHILE ON VACATION IN **BERMUDA** THAT PREVIOUS JANUARY AND CAME HOME TO **STATEN ISLAND** WITH RACQUETS, BALLS, AND NETS.

MARY'S BROTHER, EMILIUS, ARRANGED FOR HER TO SET UP A NET AND MARK OUT A TENNIS COURT ON THE GROUNDS OF THE STATEN ISLAND CRICKET AND BASEBALL CLUB AT CAMP WASHINGTON IN THE ST. GEORGE SECTION OF THE ISLAND.

MARY AND HER SISTER, LAURA, WERE THE FIRST TO PLAY TENNIS IN THIS COUNTRY.

TODAY, AMERICA'S FIRST TENNIS COURT IS A PARKING LOT FOR THE STATEN ISLAND FERRY.

There is no documentary evidence on the origin of professional basketball. Historians generally agree that it started in New Jersey. The Trenton basketball team had players on salary during the 1896-97 season. They started as a YMCA team but were allegedly kicked out of the building and played their games in the Masonic Temple.

Douglas' Dream Team

Trenton's opponents were college and YMCA teams in New York, Connecticut, New Jersey, Philadelphia, and the anthracite mining region of Pennsylvania.

ROBERT J. DOUGLAS, A NATIVE OF THE BRITISH WEST INDIES, EMIGRATED TO NEW YORK IN THE EARLY 1900's. HE PLAYED BASKETBALL IN AND AROUND HARLEM, AND DREAMED OF PLAYING PROFESSIONALLY.

AFRICAN-AMERICANS WERE BARRED FROM THE WHITE PRO LEAGUES IN THOSE DAYS. UNDAUNTED, MR. DOUGLAS ORGANIZED THE **FIRST BLACK PRO BASKETBALL TEAM** IN 1923. THEY WOULD SCHEDULE GAMES WITH PRO AND SEMI PRO CLUBS IN THE NEW YORK AREA.

I'LL CALL THEM **THE SPARTANS**

NEXT, HE TRIED TO FIND A HOME COURT.

AH...ER...OUR COURT IS ALL BOOKED UP.

YOU'VE GOT A **DEAL!**

THEN HE APPROACHED THE MANAGER OF THE RENAISSANCE CASINO IN HARLEM.

IF WE CAN PLAY OUR HOME GAMES IN THIS BALLROOM, I'LL NAME THE TEAM AFTER THE CASINO.

THAT WAS THE BEGINNING OF ONE OF THE MOST SUCCESSFUL AND POPULAR PROFESSIONAL BASKETBALL TEAMS IN THE COUNTRY DURING THE 1920's AND 30's ~ **THE RENAISSANCE BIG FIVE!**

Sportswriters often refer to basketball players as "cagers" and will give the "cage" scores. The term originated with the Trenton team who built a wire cage around their court to keep the ball from going out of bounds.

The *Rens* On the Road

THEY WERE SUCCESSFUL FROM THEIR VERY FIRST TIP-OFF IN 1923.

IN THEIR FIRST SEASON THE RENAISSANCE BIG FIVE OF HARLEM WON 38 OUT OF 48 GAMES.

THEIR POPULARITY PEAKED DURING THE DEPRESSION YEARS OF THE 1930'S. EVERY SEASON, FROM NOVEMBER TO MID APRIL, THIS AFRICAN-AMERICAN PROFESSIONAL TEAM WAS CONSTANTLY ON THE ROAD. THEY TRAVELED AS FAR WEST AS KANSAS CITY WITH OCCASIONAL FORAYS INTO THE DEEP SOUTH.

DESPITE THEIR TRIUMPHS ON THE BALL COURT, THESE ATHLETES HAD TO ENDURE PREJUDICE AND HUMILIATION, EVEN IN NORTHERN STATES.

THERE'S A REST'RAUNT DOWN THE STREET WHERE YOU FELLAS C'N EAT IN THE KITCHEN.

THE PLAYERS OFTEN RODE FAR INTO THE NIGHT TO FIND A PLACE TO SLEEP BECAUSE MANY HOTELS IN THE MIDWEST REFUSED TO ACCOMMODATE THEM.

NEVERTHELESS, THE RENAISSANCE BIG FIVE PLAYED 130 GAMES A SEASON AND WON AN AVERAGE OF EIGHTY PERCENT OF THEM.

In 1939 the *Chicago Herald* held the first of what would turn out to be ten annual World Tournaments. Each year twelve to sixteen of the best pro basketball teams competed in Chicago Stadium for the world title. Champions of various leagues and the black independents were also invited. The winners of that first Tourney were the Rens.

THE RENAISSANCE BIG FIVE

PLAYED THEIR HOME GAMES AT THE RENAISSANCE CASINO IN HARLEM TWICE A YEAR—DURING THE THANKSGIVING AND CHRISTMAS HOLIDAYS. ONLY ONE TEAM EVER BEAT THEM IN THE CASINO, THE PHILADELPHIA SPHAS, AN ALL-JEWISH TEAM.

ROBERT DOUGLAS OWNER-MANAGER

WHILE ON THE ROAD, THE RENS CONSISTED OF SEVEN OR EIGHT PLAYERS, THE MANAGER, AND THE BUS DRIVER.

SHOWN HERE IS THE RENS' TEAM THAT RACKED UP THE BEST RECORD OF ANY PROFESSIONAL BASKETBALL CLUB IN THE U.S. DURING THE 1932-33 SEASON. OUT OF 128 GAMES THEY WON 120 AND COMPILED AN 88-GAME WINNING STREAK.

"FATS" JENKINS WAS PROBABLY THE **HIGHEST PAID** PLAYER, MAKING **$225** A WEEK.

"PAPPY" RICKS

BILL YANCEY

EYRE SAITCH WAS ALSO A TOP-RANKING TENNIS PLAYER

JOHN HOLT

"WEE WILLIE" SMITH 6 FT. 5 IN. CENTER

SMITH AND COOPER WERE THE ONLY ONES OVER SIX FEET TALL ON THIS ROSTER

THE BIG FIVE MOVED TO OHIO IN THE 1940'S AND BECAME THE DAYTON RENS. WHEN THEY DISBANDED IN 1949, THEIR 26-SEASON RECORD STOOD AT 2,318 VICTORIES AND 381 LOSSES.

"TARZAN" COOPER 6 FT. 3 IN.

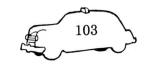

Pro basketball took root in the US in 1898 with the advent of the National Basketball League. It fell apart in 1903. Over the next half century there were dozens of pro leagues all over the country. Another organization calling itself the National Basketball League (NBL) was formed in 1937 and it employed a few African-Americans during World War II.

COOPER, CLIFTON, & LLOYD

A Competitor of the NBL, the Basketball Association of America (BAA), was started in 1946. Three years later, the NBL and BAA merged and called themselves the National Basketball Association.

RACIAL INTEGRATION CAME TO THE NATIONAL BASKETBALL ASSOCIATION DURING THE COLLEGE DRAFT OF 1950. BOSTON CELTICS OWNER WALTER BROWN SELECTED **CHUCK COOPER** OF DUQUESNE UNIVERSITY IN THE SECOND ROUND.

ON THE NINTH ROUND THE **WASHINGTON CAPITOLS** DRAFTED **EARL LLOYD** OUT OF **WEST VIRGINIA STATE COLLEGE**.

HOWEVER, A FEW HOURS **AFTER** THE DRAFT, **NAT CLIFTON**, THE 6'7" CENTER FROM THE HARLEM GLOBETROTTERS, BECAME THE FIRST AFRICAN-AMERICAN TO ACTUALLY SIGN A FORMAL NBA CONTRACT

NEW YORK KNICKERBO

BUT IT WAS THE LEAGUE SCHEDULE WHICH DETERMINED WHO WOULD BE THE FIRST AFRICAN-AMERICAN TO TASTE ACTION IN AN NBA GAME. EARL LLOYD PLAYED IN WASHINGTON'S SEASON OPENER AGAINST THE ROCHESTER ROYALS ON OCTOBER 31, 1950.

OF THESE THREE PIONEERS, EARL LLOYD REMAINED IN THE LEAGUE THE LONGEST, TEN YEARS. CLIFTON STAYED EIGHT YEARS AND RACKED UP OVER 5,000 CAREER POINTS.

General Index

105